PREFACE

This booklet was preceded by two others, "What Catholics Believe", (The Apostles Creed) and "The Seven Sacraments". All of these booklets try to present Catholic teaching in a clear and easy to read format.

Although the Catholic Catechism was consulted after the original drafts of each commandment to ensure the accuracy and inclusion of all essential topics, this booklet does not attempt to be a summary of the Catechism. On some specialized issues such as artificial insemination, end-of-life questions, the Church's theory of a just war and her social justice principles, the Catechism is quoted directly.

Also, this booklet is not a short compendium of moral theology. Its purpose is to clarify obligations, to motivate and to instruct. Scriptural quotes comprise a large portion of every chapter, because getting the biblical roots provides a solid foundation and a powerful attraction to goodness.

Protestant Enumeration

Protestant Churches separate the first commandment into two parts and join commandments 9 and 10. As a result, the numbering differs (e.g. The Catholic second commandment is the Protestant third commandment, etc.)

TABLE OF CONTENTS

INTRODUCTION

The Ten Commandments are making headline news. The breakdown in American morality has sparked a grassroots movement to restore the Ten Commandments. Religious groups place them in public school classrooms and some government officials display them in their offices. Legal battles over these actions will probably be decided by the Supreme Court.

Jewish and Christian

Because rooted in the Old Testament, the Ten Commandments are the religious heritage of both the Jewish and Christian communities. Even non-believers see their importance as the basic foundation for morality.

IMPORTANCE AND LIMITATIONS

Importance

People need to know how they should live. They need clear ideals. Unfortunately, Americans want to be free. They like ambiguity in moral issues. They don't like anyone, including God, telling them what to do. Yet, clarity is especially needed when sinful tendencies must be curtailed.

Limitations

Unfortunately, knowing the commandments doesn't guarantee the keeping of the commandments. The Catholic Church teaches clearly about original sin and the power of evil within everyone. There is also the tremendous power of the world culture and the presence of the devil.

The Struggle and the Victory

St. Paul writes clearly of his inner struggles, "I cannot even understand my own actions. I do not do what I want to do but what I hate." (Rom. 7:15). Paul found the answer to this struggle in the power of Jesus Christ. "Who can free me from this body under the power of death? All praise to God, through Jesus Christ." (Rom. 7:24-25) May your own struggle to keep these commands lead you to faith in Jesus and to your victory through Jesus Christ. (1Cor.15:57)

I

FOR ALL PEOPLE

For Jew and Gentile
Although these Ten Commandments were originally given in a Jewish context, they have been accepted fully into Christ's teaching. St. Paul writes, they are "now made known to all the Gentiles that they may believe and obey." (Rom. 16:26)

Especially for the Believer
The greatest motive for keeping the commandments is faith in God. A powerful faith should result in the person's commitment to these commandments. All religious denominations have this link between faith and moral uprightness.

Even For Non-Believers
Although revealed in the Bible, these commandments are written inside every human person. Paul writes, "In fact, whatever can be known about God, is clear to them; He Himself made it so." Paul's conclusion is: "Therefore these men are inexcusable." (Rom.1:19-20)

Personal Responsibility
No one can say "I don't belong to any religion," or "I don't believe in God." The Ten Commandments are written inside every human person. These words are not meant to crush but to encourage.

The Great Invitation
Inside every human person is a deep need for God's friendship and an understanding of the responsibilities involved in that personal relationship. Accepting God and His commandments allows the person to grasp the great invitation of human life, namely to search and to find the God who created us.

Needed Direction
Every American, after buying something new, reads the directions because they want to know how to use it correctly and how to avoid ruining their new high-priced possession. These commandments help us not to ruin our lives. They contain a wisdom which needs to be acquired at the very beginning of life.

II

Very Important to God

Many people treat these commandments as if they were "the Ten Suggestions". However, God considers them extremely important. Let's examine Exodus:19, 9-25 which describes the scene. The Israelites are three months into the desert (very early in the journey). When they arrive at Mount Sinai, God tells the people to prepare for the special third day when He Himself will come down. This mountain is so holy, that no one can approach except Moses. All must abstain from intercourse for three days.

On the day itself there are peals of thunder and lighting, a heavy cloud and a trumpet blast, "so that all the people in the camp trembled." Sinai was wrapped in smoke and "the smoke rose from it as though from a furnace." The whole mountain trembled violently. After that, God summoned Moses to the top of the mountain and delivered all the commandments.

These signs show that God wants us to take these commandments very seriously.

Sin

1. Sin is any thought, word, action or omission which violates God's commandments.
2. A person actually commits a sin (called subjective sin) when they know that their thought, word, action or omission is against God's law and they freely consent. In these cases, they are culpable (able to be blamed).
3. However, some sins (called objective sin) are not culpable because the person is not aware that their thoughts, words, actions or omissions are sinful, or they did not act freely.
4. The Catholic Church teaches that there are two kinds of sin – mortal (grievous) and venial (less serious).
5. These questions of right and wrong, serious or not serious, should be submitted by Catholics to the priest in confession.

Society and Sin

1. Modern society has tried to wipe away the very idea of sin.

III

2. This attempt has had serious harmful consequences, because society has refused to face the deep complexities of the human person.

Guilt
1. Guilt is an important feeling of the human spirit, just as physical pain is an important signal within the human body.
2. A true and healthy guilt arises when a person has done something wrong and honestly accepts responsibility.
3. Attempts are often made to repress guilt feelings but this approach leads to emotional problems.
4. God has provided both human and spiritual means of ridding ourselves of guilt feelings.

Forgiveness
1. On a human level, God has provided the gift of speech, whereby we can seek forgiveness from others.
2. On the supernatural level, the Bible contains promises of God's forgiveness, and means to attain that forgiveness.
3. Catholics use their gift of speech in the Sacrament of Reconciliation (Confession). They receive forgiveness through the Church's priest after a confession of sins.
4. There is no need for anyone at anytime, no matter what sins have been committed, to feel trapped in their guilt. While still on earth, we live in a time of God's mercy.

Conscience
1. Human conscience is the rational power to judge whether sin has been committed or not. Conscience also judges whether sin has been forgiven or not.
2. Just as a little infant attempting to walk finds within a surprise power of balance, so God has placed in every human being this rational power called human conscience.
3. The forming of conscience begins at birth, through the parents, the first teachers of their children.

4. Conscience, like any human power, is not always correct. In fact, the same person within their lifetime, might change their judgement about what is sinful or not. (For example, some doctors who performed abortions now speak out for pro-life.)
5. Because so much depends upon rightly formed consciences, God gave us the Ten Commandments
6. Without a correctly formed conscience, the person does not realize his/her duties to spouse, children, friends or to society itself.

Culture and Conscience
1. Conscience is not the result of a culture, but is greatly formed by cultural factors.
2. The mass media, especially in the modern world, exerts a tremendous power in forming what people see as sinful or not sinful.
3. With poorly formed consciences, we cannot limit the inner evil of the person or the collective evil within society. All becomes personal destruction and anarchy.

The Ten Commandments
1. Standing as gigantic safety barriers, preventing persons and societies from plunging over the cliff of self-destruction are those ten important sentences which speak so clearly.
2. The Ten Commandments are not limits destroying self-fulfillment. They are guidelines so we don't lose our way.
3. Just as children mature and see the value of "coloring within the lines", so a mature human person attempts to live within God's lines

The "Goal"
As in my two other booklets (on the Apostles Creed and the Seven Sacraments), my only goal is to explain God's gift of the Ten Commandments as simply as possible.

ADVICE OF TOBIT TO HIS SON, TOBIAH

Through all your days, my son, keep the Lord in mind, and suppress every desire to sin or to break his commandments. Perform good works all the days of your life, and do not tread the paths of wrongdoing.

Give alms for your possessions. Do not turn your face away from any of the poor, and God's face will not be turned away from you.

Do not keep with you overnight the wages of any man who works for you, but pay him immediately. If you thus behave as God's servant, you will receive your reward. Keep a close watch on yourself, my son, in everything you do, and discipline yourself in all your conduct. Do to no one what you yourself dislike. Do not drink wine till you become drunk, nor let drunkenness accompany you on your way.

Give to the hungry some of your bread, and to the naked some of your clothing. Whatever you have left over, give away as alms; and do not begrudge the alms you give.

Seek counsel from every wise man, and do not think lightly of any advice that can be useful. At all times bless the Lord God, and ask him to make all your paths straight and to grant success to all your endeavors and plans.

So now, my son, keep in mind my commandments, and never let them be erased from your heart.

(Excerpts from Tobit 4:5-19)

TOBIAH'S REPLY TO HIS FATHER

"Everything that you have commanded me, father, I will do."

(5:2)

FIRST COMMANDMENT

Part 1
"I am the Lord your God" (Exodus 20: 2)

Seeking God

1. No one is excused from the deepest inner movement of the human heart - to know and love the living God.
2. The centuries have shown clearly (like wisdom fully displayed) that people who seek God, and fulfill this First Commandment, are the same ones who find meaning in their lives and offer to help others.

Made for God

1. Although friendships and relationships help alleviate man's greatest suffering (the loneliness of the human heart) a great mystery remains.
2. No matter how deep the friendship or how loving the relationship, human loneliness is not totally quenched by human friendship.
3. "Other people" are human like ourselves. They did not make us. They did not create us. They cannot fully satisfy us.
4. The Bible invites us to a friendship with God, for whom alone our hearts were made.

The Gift of Faith

1. Most Americans have heard about God.
2. Many received their faith in childhood.
3. Preserving that faith into adulthood helps the person to understand and cope with human life.
4. There are also special "faith" moments, when the person experiences the loving and helping Person of the heavenly Father.

Vocal Prayer

1. Every Jewish synagogue and every Christian church has prayers, words helping us speak to God.

1

2. These prayers were often composed directly under God's inspiration (as the Psalms).
3. These prayers are only the beginning step.
4. God invites everyone into a deep, personal relationship.

Personal Prayer
1. The Catholic Church has a much deeper prayer stream, beginning with a prayer gift called "fervor".
2. By this "fervor" gift, God breaks into the person's mind and feelings.
3. Having received this "fervor" gift, the believer begins to experience the presence of God.
4. For Christians, this breakthrough is always through the humanity of Jesus.

Explaining the Breakthrough
1. This breakthrough is called "being born again" or "being baptized in the Spirit".
2. Although these are not Catholic phrases, the Church has a 2000 year tradition of this conversion experience, leading to the "prayer of the heart".
3. All should know and seek this gift, "Ask and you shall receive". (Mt. 7:7)
4. This prayer gift is not meant to pass away, but to deepen and grow.

False Religious Searching
1. Modern America is in the midst of a gigantic religious searching.
2. Technology is seen clearly as a "false god" which cannot deliver the personal fulfillment which comes from God alone.
3. Unfortunately, this spiritual searching has led many into the occult and into false religions (enumerated in Part 2 of this commandment).
4. This searching should lead to a true spiritual relationship with Jesus as Lord.

The Covenant

1. This first sentence, "I am the Lord, your God" is extremely important because all the other commandments flow from a special invitation of God called a Covenant.
2. The Bible tells a very simple story. God wants to reestablish a relationship with the human race which was broken by man's sin. God calls this new relationship a Covenant.

The Covenant Beginnings

1. This Covenant begins with Noah and its sign is the rainbow. (Gen. C9)
2. The Noah Covenant is renewed with Abraham, a name meaning, "The Father of many nations." (Gen. C15)
3. God tells Abraham, "My covenant with you is this: you are to become the father of a host of nations." (Gen.17:4)
4. The sign of this covenant is circumcision. (17:11)

The New Covenant

1. While keeping continuity with the Old Covenant, Jesus established a new Covenant in His blood. (Mt.26:28; Mk. 14:24; Lk. 23:24)
2. The Covenant of Noah, Abraham and the New Covenant of Jesus are totally gifts from God.

Moral Demands

1. The Bible speaks clearly of the moral demands of these Covenants, constantly explaining what is required of the believer to stand in the holiness of God.
2. Although the Ten Commandments do not exhaust the radical demands of the Covenant, they do constitute a clear expression of basic, non-negotiable demands that God requires.
3. In fact, their structure resembles a treaty made between a lord and his subjects, outlining the basic requirements for them to enjoy his protection.

PART 2
"You shall not have other gods before me."
(Exodus 20:3)

Duty to Seek God
1. Every human person has a God-given task and goal for their life.
2. The task or the work, however, is not God.
3. Every person's primary task is to seek and find God.
4. Faith in God helps many to find what their task is and to fulfill God's purpose.

False Gods
1. Unfortunately, due to inner drives and ambitions, as well as a false value system (whereby a person's worth is measured by their salary or position), human career goals replace the living God as Lord, leading to a false worship.
2. Caught in these false systems, many forget their inner call to seek God.

ATHEISM AND AGNOSTICISM

1. There is a serious modern problem of non-belief in God's existence.
2. This problem can be attributed to the breakdown of the family, which nourished faith in the children.
3. This problem is also rooted in the American cultural upheaval. Our culture is no longer formed by biblical teachings.
4. Culture, might explain the reasons for non-belief but every person still has the responsibility of asking, "Is there a God and how can I know Him?"
5. As a result, many people take their world-view from the mass media and from a powerful secular culture, which is now post-biblical.
6. This large number of non-believers is a challenge for the Churches who need to address this problem.

Real Powers of God
1. The Bible speaks clearly of the true supernatural powers of the Holy Spirit, which God freely bestows upon believers so they can help other people.
2. Scripture and Catholic tradition contain clear rules and guidelines for these charismatic gifts.

False Powers of Satan
1. By occult powers, Satan counterfeits God's true powers.
2. Unfortunately, in modern times, these occult powers have become popular, and highly lucrative to those who claim them
3. These powers are real. Their source is the Kingdom of Darkness (Demonic).
4. Unfortunately, America is clueless about these occult powers which now flood our mainstream culture.

CATHOLIC TEACHING ON FALSE POWERS

The Catholic Catechism teaches clearly:
1. "All forms of divination are to be rejected: recourse to Satan or demons, conjuring up the dead or other practices falsely supposed to "unveil" the future. Consulting horoscopes, astrology, palm reading, interpretation of omens and lots, the phenomena of clairvoyance and recourse to mediums." (Cat. 2116)
2. The Catechism also condemns, "All practices of magic or sorcery and wearing charms and spiritism." (Cat. 2117)

Other Doors into the Occult
1. Older forms of occult dabbling are Ouija Boards and Tarot Cards.
2. Newer forms are the New Age powers, such a crystal healing.

Old Testament
1. The Old Testament spoke frequently against divinations:
   a) "Do not practice divination or soothsaying." (Lv. 19:26)
   b) "For a sin like divination is rebellion." (1Sm.13:23)

2. The Israelites under king Ahaz are condemned: "They practiced fortune-telling and divination." (2Kg. 17:17)
3. King Manasseh is condemned because, "He practiced soothsaying and divination and reintroduced the consulting of ghosts and spirits. (1Kg.21:6 c.f. 2Chr.33:6)
4. Both Jeremiah and Ezekiel condemn the "Lying visions and false divinations." (Jer.14:14 and Ez.13:6)
5. Micah proclaims that God, "will abolish the means of divination from your use." (5:11)
6. The Book of Deuteronomy gives a detailed list: "Let there not be found among you . . . a fortune-teller, soothsayer, diviner or caster of spells, nor anyone who consults ghosts and spirits or seeks oracles from the dead. (Dt.18:10-11)

New Testament
1. At Philippi, Paul encountered a slave girl who brought "substantial profit to her masters by fortune telling by a clairvoyant spirit, which Paul commanded to leave her." (Acts 16:16)
2. Paul got into trouble because the girl lost her clairvoyant powers and her owners lost their income. (Acts16: 16-19)

Practices Based on Eastern Religions
1. Practices based on eastern religions are often rooted in the occult. Attempts to Christianize these are self-delusions.
2. Yoga and Enneagram, often used by Catholics have their roots in an eastern religion.

FALSE RELIGIONS

Non-Biblical Religions
1. American religious practice used to be based on the Bible.
2. Today, a variety of non-biblical religions propagate beliefs that violate the clear teaching of Sacred Scripture.
3. Some of these religions would be: Christian Science, Unitarianism, Swedenborgianism and Unity Churches.
4. Many other forms have sprung up using other names.

Doctrines of Non-Biblical Religions

1. A deep study reveals the basic teachings of these false religions:
   a) God is not really the Creator. The universe is just a manifestation of God.
   b) Every human person, by birth, has divine elements within.
   c) God's relationship to man is not a personal one.
   d) Life's purpose is human development, a full realization of the divine potential within each person, given at birth.
   e) If union with God is not completed here on earth, the process will continue after death.
   f) In the end, all will be reunited within God, because human persons are just manifestations of God, not distinct from Him.
2. Obviously, these teachings destroy all the biblical dogmas about God and man even though many elements of the Bible might seemingly be incorporated into the teaching.

Catholic Truths

1. The true Catholic doctrines (explained fully in my booklet on the Apostles Creed) include:
   a) God is the Creator and the universe is distinct from Him.
   b) God creates human persons because He wants a relationship with them.
   c) Because of sin, the relationship between God and the human family has been broken.
   d) God began to restore this relationship by His Covenant to Abraham.
   e) Finally, God sent Jesus as our Savior and Redeemer.
   f) Jesus' obedient death on the cross and rising from the dead has reconciled mankind to God.
   g) Jesus completed His work by sending the Holy Spirit.
   h) Anyone who believes in Jesus and is baptized becomes a temple of the Holy Spirit.

Contrast of Doctrines

1. The false religions say that by our natural birth we are one with God. Religious practice just helps us gain our human potential.

2. Catholicism teaches that we are alienated from God but that God has saved us by intervening into human history. Life with God is a gift of grace received by faith in Jesus Christ.

Jesus as Lord – The Real Test
1. All of the false practices and false religions would accord Jesus some role but would never proclaim Him as Lord, equal to the Father.
2. St. Paul says clearly that the Holy Spirit leads everyone to proclaim "Jesus is Lord". (1Cor.12:3)
3. Dabbling in spiritual powers without Jesus as Lord is extremely dangerous.
4. All true and valid religious powers are under Jesus' authority.

Summary
1. "I am the Lord your God" states that God wants to make a covenant with us.
2. Not having false gods clears away obstacles to that covenant.

SECOND COMMANDMENT

"You shall not take the name of the Lord, your God, in vain.
For the Lord will not leave unpunished him who
takes His name in vain." (Ex. 20:7)
(This command is repeated in LV. 19:12, 22:32 and Dt.5:11)

Importance of Human Name
1. Each person's name is unique. By their name, a person identifies himself/herself and is identified by others.
2. Remembering a person's name is a unique token of respect.
3. Reviling their name is a personal injury.

Bestowal of Names in the Bible

1. God frequently bestowed a new name upon His chosen servants, for example, Abraham (Gen.17:5), Israel (Gen.32:24) and Peter (Jn.1:42)
2. The Christian name is even more significant because it is received in Baptism and conferred in the name of the Trinity.
3. The Book of Revelation refers frequently to the Christian's new name. When the victory is won, our names will be:
   a) written on a white stone (2:17)
   b) never be erased from the book of life (3:5)
   c) share in Jesus' new name (3:12)
4. Revelation even promises that the victors will bear Jesus' name on their foreheads. (22:4)

OLD TESTAMENT

God's Name in Scripture

1. God's very first name in Scripture was "Shaddai" (used in Genesis and older biblical poems.), translated "Almighty" but literally means, "the One of the Mountain."
2. Later names are El and Elohim, which are frequently followed by a defining phrase El of Israel (the God of Israel).
3. The personal name of Israel's God is Yahweh, meaning, "I am who am".
4. Yahweh is clearly Israel's God and needs no other defining word.

God's Name

1. In the Bible, knowing God's name brings closeness and intimacy. To some degree, it allows the person to influence God.
2. Four times, Genesis says explicitly that Abraham "invoked the Lord by name." (12:8, 13:4, 21:33 and 26:25)
3. The most famous biblical moment is when Moses is bold enough to ask God His name, "If they ask me, 'What is his name?' What am I to tell them?"
4. God's response was, "This is what you shall tell the Israelites: I Am sent me to you." (Ex.3:14)

Power and Presence of God's Name
1. David knew the power in God's name. "You (Goliath) come against me with sword and spear and scimitar ... but I come against you in the name of the Lord of hosts." (1Sam. 17: 45)
2. When Solomon consecrated the temple, God said, "I confer my name upon it forever." (1Kg. 9:3)

Wrong Use of God's Name
1. A man quarreling with another, "blasphemed the Lord's name" and was stoned to death. (Lv. 24:10-16)
2. The Bible says, "Whoever blasphemes the name of the Lord shall be put to death." (Lv. 24:16)
3. A prophet using God's name falsely, is also under a death penalty. "If a prophet presumes to speak in my name an oracle that I have not commanded him to speak, he shall die." (Dt. 18:20)

NEW TESTAMENT

Name of Jesus
1. God Himself chose Jesus' name, revealing this:
    a) To Joseph –"You are to name him Jesus because He will save his people from their sins." (Mt.1:21)
    b) To Mary – "You will conceive and bear a son and give him the name Jesus." (Lk. 1:31)
2. The gospels mention the great power of Jesus' name.
    a) doing miracles
      "Did we not do many miracles in your name?" (Mt. 7:22)
    b) expelling demons
      "Teacher, we saw a man using your name to expel demons." (Mk.9:38)
3. Jesus Himself proclaims the power of His own name.
      "They will use my name to expel demons." (Mk. 16:17)
4. Jesus made promises about His name:
    a) "Where two or three are gathered in my name, there am I in their midst." (Mt.18:20)
    b) "Whatever you ask in my name, I will do." (Jn. 14:13)

5. After Pentecost, the apostles use Jesus' name:
   a) Peter explains the power used in healing the lame man. "It was done in the name of Jesus Christ the Nazarene." (Acts 4:10)
   b) Paul casts out the demon in the slave girl. "In the name of Jesus Christ I command you, come out of her." (Acts 16:18)

Saving Power of Jesus' Name

1. The saving power of Jesus' name is stated often in the New Testament:
   a) "There is no other name in the whole world given to men by which we are to be saved." (Acts 4:12)
   b)"Then shall everyone be saved who calls on the name of the Lord." (Acts 2:21)
   c) "Everyone who calls on the name of the Lord will be saved." (Rom 10:13)
   d) "Through his Name your sins have been forgiven." (1Jn. 2:12)
2. Jesus' authority over the angels is reflected in His name. Jesus is "far superior to the angels as the name He has inherited is superior to theirs." (Heb.1:4)

The Greatness of the Name

The Christian hymn, preserved for us by St. Paul proclaims Jesus' name:

"Because of this,
God highly exalted him
and bestowed on him the name
above every other name,
So that at Jesus' name
every knee must bend
in the heavens, on the earth,
and under the earth,
and every tongue proclaim
to the glory of God the Father:
Jesus Christ is Lord!" (Ph.2:10-11)

Jesus' Teaching

1. Jesus is very strict concerning God's name in oaths: "What I tell you is: do not swear at all. Do not swear by heaven...nor by earth...nor by Jerusalem." (Mt.5:34-35)
2. James echoes Jesus' teaching:
   "Above all else, my brothers, you must not swear an oath, any oath at all, either 'by heaven' or 'by earth'". (5:12)

Paul's Interpretation

1. On some occasions of serious consequence, Paul himself wanted God as a witness:
   a) "I call on God as my witness that it was out of consideration for you that I did not come to Corinth again." (2Cor.1:23)
   b) "I declare before God that what I have just written is true." (Gal.1:20)
2. Following St. Paul, the Church states that oaths can be made in serious circumstances or when required by legitimate authority.

PRACTICAL APPLICATION

Profanity and Blasphemy

1 Both profanity and blasphemy are sins in which a person "uses God's name in vain."
2 By profanity a person uses God's name from a careless and inappropriate speech pattern.
3 Blasphemy is more serious because the person treats God with deliberate irreverence and contempt.
4 By blasphemy a person either:
   a) deliberately attacks the honor of God with an intent to insult God, or
   b) invokes God's name in a curse against another human being

Perjury

1. At a certain solemn moment, as testimony in a trial, an oath is rightfully required.

2. Perjury is to take an oath with the intention to deceive, or to lie under questioning.

Conclusion
1. Reverence for God demanded by the Bible must be shown by our speech.
2. Unfortunately, our culture no longer fears to use God's name in vain. The mass media has violated what used to be so sacred.
3. Today, people seem to have no fear of lying under oath.
4. Because speech patterns are formed by the culture, a true conversion experience requires changes in our use of words.
5. An inner change of heart brings about changes in speech because the person wants God's name to be praised and exalted.

THIRD COMMANDMENT

"Remember to keep holy the sabbath day" (EX.20:8)

Biblical Picture
Both the Old and New Testament give an extensive picture of the need to keep holy the sabbath. For Christians, the sabbath holiness has been transferred to Sunday due to Jesus rising from the dead. Although the days vary (Saturday and Sunday), the basic reverence for the Lord's day is required by Jew and Christian.

OLD TESTAMENT

God's Command
1. The idea of the sabbath being holy is rooted deeply in the Old Testament.
2. So God blessed the seventh day and made it holy, because on it he rested from all the work he had done in creation. (Gen. 2:3)
3. God commanded that no Israelite collect manna on the sabbath. (Ex. 16:23)

4. Shortly after that, God gave the explicit command, "Remember to keep holy the sabbath day". (Ex.20:8 and Deut.5:12)
5. God notes the reason for this command: "In six days the Lord made the heavens and the earth, the sea and all that is in them; but on the seventh day he rested. (Ex.20:11)
6. God clearly commands both rest and worship on the sabbath.

Rest
1. The Lord said to Moses, "On the seventh day everyone is to stay home and no one is to go out. After that the people rested on the seventh day." (Ex.16:29-30)
2. "You shall not even light a fire in any of your dwellings on the sabbath day." (Ex.35:3)

Worship
1. "But the seventh day is the sabbath rest, a day for the sacred assembly". (Lev.23:3)
2. "From one sabbath to another, all mankind shall come to worship before me, says the Lord." (Is. 66: 23)

Perpetual Command
1. "The sabbath shall belong to the Lord wherever you dwell." (Lv.23:3)
2. "This is a perpetual statute for you. You shall do no work but shall keep a sabbath of complete rest." (Lev. 23: 31, 32)

Death Penalty
1. This sabbath command is so important, that God had Moses use the death penalty. "Therefore, you must keep the sabbath as something sacred. Whoever desecrates it shall be put to death." (Ex 31:14 and 35:2)

Prophetic Voices
Because the Israelites did not keep the sabbath, the prophets became forceful in their preaching:
1. Amos speaks against those who ask when the sabbath is over "that we may display the wheat." (8:5)

2. Isaiah:
   a) praises the person "Who keeps the sabbath free from profanation." (56: 2 and 6)
   b) also says, "If you hold back your foot on the sabbath from following your own pursuits on my holy day . . . then you shall delight in the Lord." (58:13-14)
3. Jeremiah gives a clear command: "As you love your lives, take care not to carry burdens on the sabbath day . (17:21) Do no work whatever, but keep holy the sabbath." (17:22)
4. Jeremiah even prophesies that Jerusalem would not be destroyed, if people would just keep the sabbath. Unfortunately, nobody listened and Jerusalem was destroyed. (587 B.C.)
   a) "If you . . . carry no burden through the gates of the city on the sabbath, keeping the sabbath holy and abstaining from all work on it . . . this city will remain inhabited forever." (17:24-25)

Old Testament
1. Old Testament Judaism frequently needed reform. Especially important are the reforms of Nehemiah (about 450 B.C.) and the reform under the Maccabees (about 150 B.C.).
2. Both of these reform movements restored the sabbath rest.

Nehemiah Reform
1. "When the peoples of the land bring in merchandise or any kind of grain for sale on the sabbath day, we will not buy from them on the sabbath or on any holyday." (Neh 10:32)
2. Nehemiah had a gigantic confrontation with "the nobles of Judah", blaming the entire destruction of Jerusalem on this evil. "Did not your fathers act in this same way, with the result that our God has brought all this evil upon us and upon this city." (Neh.13: 18)

Reform of the Maccabees
1. In the second century before Jesus, Judaism again needed reform:

"They sacrificed to idols and profaned the sabbath."
(1Mac.1:43)
2. The Book of Maccabees praises those Jews who so loved the sabbath that they refused even to defend themselves. (1Mac 31-38)
3. Later, even though a great victory could be won, the Maccabean army did not pursue the enemy of the sabbath.
"They observed the sabbath with fervent praise and thanks to the Lord." (2Mac8:27)

Conclusion
The importance of the sabbath for rest and worship is an extremely important element in Jewish religion. When the Israelites observed the sabbath, they did not forget the God who had saved them.

NEW TESTAMENT

Jesus
1. Jesus kept the sabbath:
   a) All four gospels speak of Jesus entering the synagogue on the sabbath. (Mt.12:9, Mk.1:21, Lk.4:16 and Jn.6:59)
   b) Luke states clearly that Jesus regularly went to the synagogue: "He came to Nazareth where he had been reared, and entering the synagogue on the sabbath as he was in the habit of doing..." (4:16)

Disciples of Jesus
1. The women at Jesus' death even waited a full day before attending to His body. "Then they went home to prepare spices and perfumes. They observed the sabbath as a day of rest, in accordance with the law. (Luke 23:56)

Disputes Over the Sabbath
1. Jesus corrected false interpretations of sabbath law, stressing that God wanted people blessed on the sabbath.
   a) "The sabbath was made for man, not man for the sabbath." (Mk.2:27)

b) Jesus healed the man with the shriveled hand on the sabbath (Mk 3: 1-6) and the man with dropsy. (Lk.14: 1-6)
2. Jesus' curing on the sabbath became a cause of persecution. "It was because Jesus did things such as this (healing) on the sabbath that they began to persecute Him." (Jn.5:16 cf Jn.7:23 and 9:14)
3. Jesus faithfully fulfilled the sabbath responsibilities, but He did not accept the sabbath interpretations that held back God's work.
4. Jesus responded to His critics: "My Father is at work until now, and I am at work as well." (Jn.5:17)

Sunday Eucharist
1. The early Church celebrated Eucharist on Sunday, because Jesus rose on that day.
2. All four gospels say clearly that Jesus rose on Sunday:
   a) Matthew – "as the first day of the week was dawning." (28:1)
   b) Mark - "Very early, just after sunrise, on the first day of the week, they came to the tomb." (16:2)
   c) Luke - "On the first day of the week, at dawn, the women came to the tomb. . ." (24:1)
   d) John "Early in the morning on the first day of the week, Mary Magdalene came to the tomb." (20:1)
3. This "first day of the week" was very special to the early Christians, because it is mentioned in all four gospels.

The Apostles Follow Jewish Practices
1. The apostles continued to worship as Jews. The first recorded healing took place, "when Peter and John were going up to the temple for prayer". (Acts 3:1-10)
2. Paul spent much of his time in synagogues on the sabbath. "Every sabbath, in the synagogue, Paul led discussions in which he persuaded certain Jews and Greeks". (Acts 18:4)

Eucharistic Celebration
1. After Pentecost, although the apostles continued Jewish practices, the early church in Jerusalem gathered regularly for

Christian Eucharist. "They devoted themselves to the apostles' instruction and the communal life, to the breaking of the bread and the prayers." (Acts 2:43)

2. St. Paul at Troas celebrated the Eucharistic meal on Sunday. "On the first day of the week, when we gathered for the breaking of the bread." (Acts 20:7)

Early Church Writings

Christian writers attest to this Sunday celebration:

1. "On the Lord's day we come together and break bread and give thanks (offer the Eucharist), after confessing our sins that our sacrifice might be pure." (The Didache 14:11 – 90 A.D.)

2. "Christians no longer observe the sabbath but live in the observance of the Lord's day on which our life rose again." (St. Ignatius of Antioch's Letter to the Magnesians: 107A.D.)

3. St Justin (martyred in Rome, 165 A.D.) gave a detailed explanation of the Sunday worship of Christians in Rome, which fits exactly the pattern of our present liturgy.

4. St. Justin writes: "On Sunday, we have a common assembly of all our members. We hold our common assembly on Sunday because it is the first day of the week, and because on that same day, our savior Jesus Christ rose from the dead."

Mass Attendance

1. For Catholics, Sunday devotion centers on Mass attendance. The letter to the Hebrews states: "We should not absent ourselves from the assembly, as some do, but encourage one another." (10:25)

2. Mass is important because only in Church can the person receive the Body and Blood of Christ, a devotion surrounded by Jesus' promises of everlasting life. (Jn.6:53-58) (Confer my booklet on the Seven Sacraments.)

3. Jesus promised to raise up to eternal life those who feed on His flesh and drink His blood. (Jn.6:54)

4. In practice, when a Catholic experiences a need for God, they begin again to attend Mass.

18

5. Although Sunday Eucharist alone is not enough, regular attendance at Mass is the primary way of maintaining a life with God and of not succumbing to the secular culture.

Other Responsibilities
1. Even devout Catholics who attend Sunday Mass, often just live according to the American culture, shopping on Sunday and using the day for personal pursuits.
2. A full keeping of this commandment requires Catholics to examine all that they do on Sunday.
3. Also, the parish must provide opportunities for the faithful to use Sunday for spiritual growth.
4. Catholic parishes should examine other churches who invite their people to spend more time with the Church community on Sunday.

Sunday Rest and American Culture
1. The Bible provides an extensive picture of sabbath rest and worship. Modern America should heed this clarity and face the importance of God's demand for one day dedicated to Him.
2. Unfortunately, the American business community sees time as money. Sunday is violated by shopping as usual, and, in more recent years, television programming that is totally secular and pervasive.
3. Because God is seemingly powerless even on His own day, people feel very little respect for God.
4. They have lost a clear understanding of God's importance because His special day means nothing.
5. People have also lost the needed rest cycle in their week.
6. Overcoming this American Sunday culture requires a strong counter-cultural movement by the individual, the family and the parish that Sunday become the Lord's Day again.

FOURTH COMMANDMENT

"Honor your father and your mother, that you may have long life in the land which the Lord, your God, is giving you. " (Ex. 20:12)
(This is the only commandment with a promise attached!)

The Family Commandment
Having outlined the three basic responsibilities to God, the commandments now focus on human relationships. This fourth commandment highlights obligations within the family, extended family and even toward other authorities.

Genesis – Focus on Family
1. Genesis, the first book of scripture, roots all of its stories in a family setting, with a strong emphasis on the father's role.
2. It describes the creation of mankind in terms of the family. "That is why a man leaves his mother and father and clings to his wife, and the two of them become one body." (2:24)
3. The clear identity of the human family is outlined in the Table of Nations. (Chapter 10)

Fathers and Sons
1. Genesis is filled with deep, emotional scenes involving fathers and sons.
2. Abraham is blessed by his willingness to sacrifice his son. "Because you acted like you did in not withholding from me your beloved son, I will bless you abundantly . . . " (22: 16-17)
3. Jacob, by receiving the blessing of his father Isaac, begins his divine calling. (Chapter 27)
4. Joseph had a special relationship with his father Jacob, "Their father loved him best of all his sons." (37:4)
5. Years later, in Egypt, the now-powerful Joseph asks his brothers, "Is your father still living?" (43:7)
6. Realizing his father is still alive, Joseph says, "Hurry back, then, to my father and tell him: 'Thus says your son Joseph ... Come to me without delay'". (45:9)

7. After Jacob's death, Joseph fulfils his oath by traveling from Egypt to Canaan to bury his father. (Chapter 50)

Importance of the Family
1. In Genesis, the true God is identified as a family God of Abraham, Isaac and Jacob.
2. God's actions and revelations take place within the family.
3. The interaction of the biblical persons from Adam and Eve until the burial of Jacob are primarily within the family.
4. Obviously, the family is God's central plan.
5. Every Israelite, when bringing the basket of thanksgiving to the priest, had to recall, "My father was a wandering Aramean who went down to Egypt with a small household and lived there as an alien; there he became a nation great, strong and numerous." (Dt. 26:5)

The Commandment
1. Exodus, the Bible's second book, states the commandment clearly: "Honor your father and your mother, that you may have long life in the land which the Lord your God is giving you." (The only commandment with a promise attached.) (20:12; also Lv.5:16)
2. A death penalty accompanies any cursing of father or mother. (Ex. 21: 17)
3. Deuteronomy puts the commandment differently, "Cursed be he who dishonors his father or his mother." (27:16)
4. Leviticus reinforces this command: "Revere your mother and father." (19:3)
5. This relationship to parents is so important that Levitical priests were even allowed to make themselves ritually unclean to bury their deceased mother and father. (Lv. 21:2)

Commandment in Other Words
1. Some other texts are more picturesque:

    a) "My son, take care of your father when he is old. Grieve him not as long as he lives." (Sir. 3:12)

    b) "With your whole heart, honor your father, and your mother's birth pangs forget not." (Sir. 7:27)

Rewards for Obedience
1. The Bible also promises blessings for keeping this commandment.
   - a) "He who honors his father atones for sins." (Sir. 3:3)
   - b) "He who honors his father is gladdened by children and when he prays he is heard." (Sir. 3:51)
   - c) "Kindness to a father will not be forgotten. It will serve as a sin offering - it will take lasting root." (Sir.3:14)

Need for Parental Discipline of Children
The Old Testament realizes that training a child requires discipline:
1. "He who love his son chastises him often." (Sir.30:1)
2. "He who disciplines his son will benefit from him." (Sir.30:2)

Need for Obedience
1. "A wise son loves correction." (Prov.13:1)
2. "Observe, my son, your father's bidding, and reject not your mother's teaching." (Prov.6:20)

Failure of Fathers to Correct
Scripture gives examples of two famous fathers who failed to correct their sons.
1. The priest, Eli, was himself a good man but he failed to discipline his two sons. God, therefore, raised up Samuel as a prophet because Eli "knew his sons were blaspheming God" and "he did not reprove them". (1Sam.3:13)
2. King David had no control over his son, Adonijah, who "began to display his ambition to be king" and "acquired chariots, drivers and fifty henchmen. (1Kg.1:5)
3. The result is disastrous. A split takes place between the followers of Adonijah and Solomon, the two sons of David. Later, Solomon gains David's blessing to succeed him as king and then kills Adonijah. (1Kg.2:25)

A Close Father-Son Relationship
The book of Tobit portrays an excellent father-son relationship.
1. The deeply religious father, Tobit, is solicitous to train his son by many wise teachings.

2. Tobiah always did his father's will, including a difficult journey.
3. As a result, Tobiah finds a beautiful wife, Sarah, and his father receives a healing for his blindness.
4. Tobit's instructions to his son (4:5-19) should be given by every father to his children.

NEW TESTAMENT

1. Mary and Joseph are the model parents.
2. St. Joseph listened to God's angel on four occasions:
   1. taking Mary as his wife, even though he was not the father of her child. (Mt. 1:24)
   2. taking Mary to Bethlehem (Lk.2:1-7)
   3. taking Mary and Jesus to the safety of Egypt (Mt. 2:14)
   4. returning to the land of Israel, after King Herod's death (Mt. 2:21)
3. Luke's gospel shows Mary constantly accepting God's will:
   1. She became the mother of Jesus. (Lk. 1:38)
   2. She visited her kinswoman Elizabeth at the request of the angel. (1:39)
   3. She gave birth in a manger. (2:7)
   4. She presented Jesus in the temple, "according to the dictate of the law of the Lord". (2:24)
   5. She accepted that her own heart would be pierced by a sword. (2:35)
   6. She and Joseph went each year to the Temple for the Feast of Passover. (2:41)

Jesus' Obedience
Jesus' obedience to His parents is clearly recorded: "He went down with them and came to Nazareth, and was obedient to them." (Lk. 2.51)

Jesus' Teaching
1. Mark records an important occasion when Jesus is extremely upset because this commandment is set aside.

"If a person says to his father or mother, 'Any support you might have had from me is korban' (that is dedicated to God), you allow him to do nothing more for his father or mother. That is the way you nullify God's word." (Mk.7:11-13)

Early Church

1. The New Testament has many household codes, explaining to family members how they are to relate to one another. (Eph.5:22 – 6:4; Col.3: 18-21; Ti.2: 4-5; 1Pt.3: 1-7)
2. The household code from the Ephesians requires that:
   a) Husbands love their wives (5:25)
   b) Wives accept their husband's authority over them (5:22-24)
   c) Children obey their parents (6:1)
   d) Fathers not anger their children (6:4)
   f) Fathers give "instruction befitting the Lord." (6:4)

AMERICAN FAMILY LIFE

American Awakening

American parents are awakening to these truths embodied in the Old Testament:
   a) the importance of the father accepting responsibility for discipline and authority
   b) the nurturing role of the mother, especially in early childhood development
   c) the child's need for the parents to love one another

Pace of Life

1. Unfortunately, this awakening faces great cultural obstacles.
2. American life is too fast.
3. Family meals are a thing of the past.
4. Bonding between family members is destroyed by society's demands on parents' time.
5. In other words, parents are no longer in control of their own homes.
6. Regaining control means a radical tug of war with society.
7. America wants parents to be working, watching television or driving children to sports activities.

Importance of Family Worship
1. The pace of American life also destroys family prayer.
2. Fifty years ago, the American Catholic family was deeply influenced by Father Peyton whose theme was, "The family that prays together, stays together".
3. That saying gives parents a true wisdom.

The Blessings of Family Worship
1. Praying together begins with parents and children attending Sunday Mass.
2. Praying together means a daily time set aside for family prayer.
3. Family prayer has many beneficial helps for the parents and the family.
4. By prayer, a family places its life under Jesus as Lord. Praying together often brings about reconciliation and forgiveness.
5. Couples who pray together share a deeper intimacy and a better sexual life.

Limitations on Family Authority
1. Although the family is the "privileged community" and "the original cell of sacred life", its authority has limits.
2. Jesus taught clearly that the kingdom of God takes priority over the family, "Whoever loves father or mother, son or daughter more than me is not worthy of me." (Mt.10:37)
3. If necessary, the family relationships are to be sacrificed for the kingdom.
    "Everyone who has given up home, brothers or sisters, father or mother, wife or children, or property for my sake will receive many times as much and inherit everlasting life." (Mt.19:29)
4. Although listening to parental advice, children have the right to choose their own state in life, as led by God's Spirit.
5. Children should not obey any parental command that is against God's law.

Other Authorities
1. When God commands respect for parents, He also demands obedience to those who stand in the place of parents.
2. Paul taught respect for all authority. "Let everyone obey the authorities that are over him, for there is no authority except from God and all authority that exists is established by God." (Rom.13:1)
3. However, when civil commands violate God's law, they need not be obeyed.

Grandparents
1. Grandparents' relationships with the extended family must be fostered, with both old and young being blessed.
2. "Grandchildren are the crown of old men, and the glory of children is their parentage." (Pr.17:6)
3. St. Timothy benefited from the faith of his grandmother. Paul wrote, "I find myself thinking of your sincere faith – faith which first belonged to your grandmother Lois and to your mother Eunice ..." (2Tim.1:5)
4. In our day, it is extremely important that grandparents remain close to the family. They offer security for broken marriages and reinforcement of Christian values for intact marriages.

Catholic Education
1. The best child training is faith-based. The child should learn the bible stories at an early age, and be brought up in a Catholic culture.
2. An extremely important decision, which greatly affects the child, is the choice of a school. Whenever possible, a Catholic school should be chosen.
3. Grandparents can be a tremendous financial help during these years, and should aid the parents in paying for Catholic education.

FIFTH COMMANDMENT

"YOU SHALL NOT KILL." (EX. 20:13 AND DT.5:17)

"Human life is sacred because it involves the creative action of God and a special relationship with God that lasts forever. God alone is the Lord of life from its beginning to its end: no one can, under any circumstance, claim for himself the right directly to destroy an innocent human being." ("The Gift of Life" – Intro #5)

OLD TESTAMENT

God's Displeasure with Murder
1. Even before God gave this commandment, the Bible recorded five incidents of murder or attempted murder:
   a) Cain killed his brother Abel. (Gen. 4:8-16)
   b) Esau plotted to kill his brother Jacob. (Gen. 27 41-45)
   c) Joseph's brothers were going to kill him. Gen. C37)
   d) In Egypt, the midwives were told to kill all the newborn boys. (Ex.1: 15-16)
   e) Moses killed the Egyptian soldier who was beating an Israelite. (Ex.2:12)
2. From the very beginning, the human race shows this tendency to kill.
3. The Old Testament, on two occasions, records this commandment, "You shall not kill." (Ex.20:13 and Dt.5:17)

NEW TESTAMENT

Jesus' Teaching
1. Jesus repeated this commandment not to kill. (Mt.19:18 and Lk.18:20)
2. After quoting the commandment, "You shall not commit murder." (Mt. 5:21) Jesus went further, saying: "Everyone who grows angry with his brother shall be liable to judgement; any man who uses abusive language toward his brother shall be answerable to the Sanhedrin." (5:22)

3. Jesus speaks of murder as one of the vices flowing from within. (Mt. 7:21)
4. Jesus gave His clear model of peace and forgiveness. "Leave your gift at the altar, go first to be reconciled with your brother." (Mt.5:24)
5. Jesus Himself always forgave. "Father forgive them because they know not what they do." (Lk. 23;24)

Other New Testament
1. Paul and James write clearly about this command. "You shall not murder." (Rom. 13:9); "You shall not kill." (James 2:11)
2. Paul also teaches forgiveness, "Forgive whatever grievances you have against one another. Forgive as the Lord has forgiven you." (Col.3:13)

VIOLENCE TOWARDS OTHERS

Anger
1. Anger is an important emotion, needed to remove obstacles to the person's goal.
2. Anger becomes sinful when expressed in the wrong way or against the wrong person or in the wrong degree (going too far).
3. Anger that is allowed to go unchecked results in abusive language, unfair decisions, and even physical violence.
4. Handling anger as Jesus expects, requires the Holy Spirit who alone gives the fruits of peace and joy. (Gal.5:22)
5. The Spirit helps us to face honestly the question of the anger within.

Scandal
1. Scandal is any action, omission or teaching, that leads others to commit sin.
2. We are all "our brother's keepers".
3. Scandal is especially serious when given by the people who are teachers and leaders within the community.

Homicide
1. Homicide, a direct and intentional killing, is gravely sinful. This includes those who voluntarily cooperate.
2. Infanticide is especially grave, because committed against the most innocent of human persons.
3. Totally unacceptable is genocide, the wiping out of a people because of false nationalism.

Legitimate Defense
1. To kill someone in self-defense is not a sin, if that level of violence was needed to repel the attack.
2. At times, there is a clear duty to repel an aggressor, e.g., when attacking other innocent people.

Abortion and Infanticide
1. In Jesus' time, children had no rights.
2. The gospel stories of Jesus blessing the children were the foundation of the early Church declaring that even children had human rights.
3. The Church, (in its first Catechism, written about 90 A.D.) said clearly that abortion and infanticide were wrong. "You shall not kill the embryo by abortion and shall not cause the newborn to perish." (2:2)

Western Culture and Abortion
1. Eventually, this Christian view received acceptance in the laws of Western Culture.
2. Sadly, these Christian advances in human rights were repealed by a Supreme Court that was highly influenced by the politically powerful Women's Movement.
3. However, the tide is now shifting. More people see the need for abortion restrictions. The Pro-abortion Movement is losing power by the aging of its members.

Truth about Abortion
1. The full truth about abortions is still not being told, including the emotional problems that women suffer for the rest of their lives.

2. Harm is done to the reproductive organs by the unnatural act of abortion.
3. There are harmful effects upon the other children, and upon the marriage itself.
4. No matter what the secular laws declare, the Church has clearly taught the truth from the first century. Human life within the womb is sacred, not subject to any decision making by the parents.

Need for Laws Restricting Abortions
1. Statistics show that when abortions are easily available, a gigantic increase in the number of abortions results.
2. Restricting abortions, even in simple ways, causes the number to drop.
3. There was a great wisdom in society banning abortions. Because of these laws, pregnant women, for the most part, did what was right.

End of Life Questions
1. All know that the Church condemns physician-assisted suicides, when a doctor takes some action which brings about the death of the patient.
2. Many are not clear concerning the Church's teaching on using extraordinary means which prolong a person's life.
3. The Catechism states, "Discontinuing medical procedures that are burdensome, dangerous, extraordinary or disproportionate to the expected outcome can be legitimate." (2278)
4. "In these cases, there is an inability to impede death". (2278)
5. "This decision should be made by the patient if competent to act, or by those legally entitled" . (2278)
6. Providing food and water, even if through a tube, is not seen as an extraordinary or disproportionate means.

War
1. So many wars are now fought and the means of destruction are so great that war is a major problem.
2. The Church's "just war" theory has four criteria that should be used in deciding if a war is just:

a) The damage inflicted by the aggressor must be lasting, grave and certain.
b) All other means, besides war, have been used and are ineffective.
c) There are serious prospects of success.
d) The use of arms must not produce more harm than the evil to be eliminated.

3. This final criteria, "Not producing more harm" is extremely important because extensive bombing is now used to avoid casualties.

Other Aspects of War
1. Even when a war is just, the moral law remains in effect.
2. Indiscriminate destruction does not automatically become licit because of a just war.
3. Especially grave are acts of war that destroy whole cities or vast areas.
4. The Church has always condemned the bombing of civilians as a means of bringing peace.
5. Those deliberately renouncing all violence bear a needed witness to a society that accepts bloodshed as necessary.

Sinful Structures Resulting in Physical Harm
1. Today millions are starving. Many die of famine when the world is truly able to feed everyone.
2. Some parts of the world receive excellent health care, while many do not even have basic help.
3. These inequalities are due to sinful social structures and selfish political arrangements.
4. Too often, profits and power are the false guides of decisions.
5. Many of the free-world structures must be changed so all of God's children have enough to live.

SELF INFLICTED VIOLENCE

Besides demanding that we do no harm to others, this commandment requires respect also for ourselves and our own bodies. The following are sins of self-inflicted violence:

Suicide

1. God alone holds power over us, deciding the time when our lives should end.
2. Our society, impregnated with the culture of death, has more and more accepted the person's decision to terminate his/her own life, even accepting, in some places, physician-assisted suicide.
3. Accepting physician-assisted suicide allows a selfish society to avoid the more difficult approach of allotting funds for pain management.
4. Both the beginning and the end of human life is a mystery which must remain in God's hands, not ours.
5. The final years or months of a person's life are very important, when he/she prepares to meet God.
6. Abortion, infanticide and physician-assisted suicide are really closely linked, because man takes to himself a right which belongs only to God.

Alcohol Abuse

1. By alcohol abuse, the person does serious harm to the body and their entire life.
2. Alcoholism is an inherited disease. Therefore, anyone whose relatives (parents, siblings, aunts or uncles) are alcoholics, is very possibly also an alcoholic.
3. This disease causes no problem if the person doesn't drink.
4. Drinking triggers the disease's power, and the person has difficulty staying sober.
5. The only answer is total sobriety, a refusal to drink any alcohol.

Denial of Alcoholism

1. A saving moment comes when the person accepts the truth, "I am helpless and I need God's power to overcome the power that alcohol has in my life."
2. When alcohol is allowed to impair any important aspect of life – health, marriage finances, self-respect, employment, relationships, etc. then the person is an alcoholic.

3. Unfortunately, active alcoholism is frequently accompanied by massive doses of denial, with the alcoholic refusing to face what is clear to everyone else, namely, that he/she is an alcoholic.

Drug Abuse
1. Drug abuse is a more serious form of self-destruction than alcoholism.
2. After using drugs, the person experiences a newfound thirst for the drug experience.
3. Therefore, any person can become a drug addict.

Smoking
1. All the evidence shows that smoking is a cause of many illnesses.
2. Even though smokers say that quitting is difficult and sometimes not successful, every effort should be made to overcome this nicotine addiction.

Tattoos
1. We have become a tattooed people, following the examples established by sports and entertainment figures.
2. A tattoo proclaims a dominion over our bodies that belongs to God alone.
3. A tattoo violates the dignity of the person's body, which God never intended to be a human billboard. "Do not tattoo yourselves. I am the Lord." (Lev.19:28)

Body Piercing
1. Society now approves and promotes a multiple piercing of the body, which is really beneath human dignity.
2. Even animals should only be pierced and branded when absolutely needed.

SIXTH COMMANDMENT

"You shall not commit adultery."

Prologue

In Catholic teaching, the ninth commandment focuses on internal acts against purity and the sixth commandment on external sins. I would suggest that the ninth commandment be read first, because purity in thought and desire is needed to avoid sinful sexual activity.

Basic Catholic Teaching

1. The Church has always seen sexual activity within marriage as good, condemning heresies which would forbid sexual activity even in marriage.
2. The Church sees sexual activity outside of marriage and contraceptive sexual activity within marriage, as wrong.
3. This commandment requiring purity, both within and outside of marriage, presents tremendous challenges to a Christian life.

OLD TESTAMENT
Book of Genesis

Impure Acts

1. Genesis teaches that sexual sins caused God to rethink His entire plan of creation. "My spirit shall not remain in man forever ... His days shall comprise one hundred and twenty ". (6:3)
2. "In the eyes of God the earth was corrupt ..." (6:11)
3. Fortunately, "Noah found favor with the Lord." (6:8)
4. After Noah is saved, Sodom and Gomorrah are destroyed because of improper sexual activity. (C19)
5. The rape of Dinah, the daughter of Jacob and Leah, by Shechem, the son of Hamor, led Dinah's brothers to murder Hamor and all the males in his town. (C 34, 13-29)

Joseph – A Pure Heart

1. Genesis provides a powerful story of Joseph in Egypt overcoming temptation.

34

2. The wife of an Egyptian owner wants Joseph to have intercourse. Joseph's decision to be pure gets him thrown out of the house and into prison. This imprisonment was God's way of getting Pharaoh to learn of Joseph. (C 39)
3. As can be seen, sexual decisions, both good and bad, have a great influence in Genesis.

The Commandment and Punishment
1. Two books contain the commandment:
   "You shall not commit adultery." (Ex.20:14 and Dt. 5:18)
2. The Book of Leviticus decrees serious punishment for adulterers. "If a man commits adultery with his neighbor's wife, both the adulterer and the adulteress shall be put to death." (20:10)

Wisdom Books
These books teach clearly:
1. "He who commits adultery is a fool." (Pr.6:32)
2. "Such is the way of an adulterous woman. She eats, wipes her mouth, and says, 'I have done no wrong'" (Pr. 30:20)
3. "So also with the woman who is unfaithful to her husband... In her wanton adultery she has borne children by another man." (Sir. 24: 22-23)

Advising Young Men
The Book of Proverbs advises young men to avoid adultery:
1. "The lips of an adulteress drip with honey and her mouth is smoother than oil." (5:3)
2. "Your wife will watch over you . . . will share your concerns and will guide you. Why then, my son, should you . . . accept the embraces of an adulteress." (5:19-20)
3. "My son, keep my words . . . that they may keep you from another's wife." (7:5)

Fornication
1. The Old Testament also condemns sexual activity of single persons.

2. Prohibition against sexual activity by the unmarried is usually condemned as prostitution.
   a) "You shall not degrade your daughter by making a prostitute of her. (Lv. 19:29)
   b) "Son and father go to the same prostitute, profaning my name." (Am.2:7)
   c) The Gentiles...amused themselves with prostitutes." (2Mal.6:4)

NEW TESTAMENT

Jesus' Teaching
1. Jesus, when speaking to the rich young man, quotes this commandment, "You shall not commit adultery." (Lk. 18:20)
2. Jesus widens its scope: "You have heard the commandment, 'You shall not commit adultery.' What I say to you is: anyone who looks lustfully at a woman has already committed adultery with her in his thoughts." (Mt. 5: 27-28)
3. To the woman taken in adultery, Jesus said, "You may go now. But from now on, avoid this sin." (Jn.8:11)
4. Jesus lists fornication as one of the "wicked designs coming from the deep recesses of the heart." (Mk.7:21: Mt. 15:19)

Paul's Teaching
1. Jesus' teachings provide the basis for Paul's condemnations of adultery. (Rom.2:22 and 13:9)
2. Paul lists adulterers among those who will not inherit the kingdom. "Do not deceive yourselves: no fornicators, idolaters, no adulterers . . . will inherit God's kingdom (1Cor6: 9-10 also Eph.5:5 and Col. 3:5)
3. Paul asks repentance from sexual sins:
   "I may have to mourn over the many who sinned earlier and have not repented of the uncleanness, fornication and sensuality they practiced." (2Cor12:21)
4. Paul sees sexual sins as extremely personal.
   "Every other sin a man commits is outside his body, but the fornicator sins against his own body." (1Cor.6:18)

Effects of Adultery

1. Besides being sinful, adultery severely harms everyone involved – the two people, the spouse(s) and the children.
2. Adultery shakes the foundations of every marriage. Marriage partners have a very difficult time in forgetting what happened, even when they have forgiven their spouse.
3. Especially problematic is when adultery leads to divorce. Marriages begun by an adulterous relationship are notoriously unhappy.
4. It should be clear that adultery is always wrong, no matter what the extenuating circumstances. An unhappy home life or a spouse that doesn't fulfill expectations are no excuse.

MODERN AMERICA

Lost Innocence

God's plan, that the first and only sexual partner is the spouse, has been lost in America due to a combination of factors:

1. The absence of strong parental models leads to early promiscuity.
2. The availability of contraceptives and abortion has removed the walls placed by nature to curb premarital activity.
3. The media mocks virginity and portrays fornication as the norm.
4. Our culture refuses to face the emotional problems involved in premarital sexuality, and teaches that no emotional distress or confusion results from fornication.
5. This total emotional numbing (by the MTV culture) of American youth invites promiscuity.
6. Although the modern world still has some misgivings about adultery, it sees nothing wrong with fornication (as long as it is "safe sex").
7. Postponing marriage to a later age means that young adults need to refrain from sexual activity for many more years than was formerly true.

Why the Problem?
1. The American culture is killing Christian sexual ideals. Every aspect is involved:
    a) the booming economy
    b) the breakdown of family traditions
    c) more women in the workplace
    d) the years needed to prepare for a career
    e) contraception and abortion
    f) the emphasis on taking a "non-judgmental" stance
    g) the belief that all morality is relative and that nothing is sinful if nobody gets hurt
    h) the availability of pornography
    i) the constant bombardment, especially upon the young, of sexual images, all day and every day.

Society's Contraceptive Mentality
1. The widescale breakdown of pre-marital purity is due primarily to the moral acceptance of contraceptives.
2. Recent studies, by sociologists with no religious background, show that contraceptives and abortion have actually freed the man from responsibility and have burdened the woman who must assume the duty of "protecting herself", or "getting an abortion" if pregnancy does result.

Living Together
1. Another problem (which many times is not seen as such) is couples living together before marriage. This has increased 1000% in the last 40 years, and has become more the norm than the exception.
2. Statistics now show that living together is a very poor way to prepare for a lifelong commitment.
3. The obvious is happening. If people can fulfill their sexual desires without the burden of a marriage commitment or the possibility of pregnancy, they will choose this more selfish path with all of its consequences.

DIVORCE

Ideal of Genesis
1. The Bible's first book gives the right ideal of marriage, "That is why a man leaves his father and mother and clings to his wife, and the two of them become one body." (2:24)

Breakdown of the Ideal
1. The Old Testament, however, allows a breakdown of this ideal.
2. Even after the Ten Commandments, Moses allowed the Israelites to give a bill of divorce. (Dt. 24:1)
3. The Old Testament has many examples of multiple marriages by Kings like David and Solomon.

Restoration of the Ideal
1. Jesus obviously wanted to restore the original ideal of Genesis.
2. Jesus commented on Moses' decision, "He wrote that commandment for you because of your stubbornness." (Mk.10:5)
3. Jesus contrasts Moses' action with God's original plan in Genesis. "At the beginning of creation God made them male and female; for this reason a man shall leave his father and mother and the two shall be as one. They are no longer two but one flesh." (Mk 10: 6-8, Mt. 19: 4-6)
4. Jesus then restored the ideal. "Therefore, let no man separate what God has joined." (Mk. 10: 9, cf. Mt. 19:6)
5. Later, alone with his disciples, Jesus is even more explicit. "Whoever divorces his wife and marries another commits adultery against her; and the woman who divorces her husband and marries another commits adultery." (Mk.10:11-12 and Lk.16:18)

Matthew's Exception
1. Matthew's gospel adds a phrase to Jesus' teaching on divorce, "lewd conduct is a separate case". (19:9)
2. Catholic scholars see this phrase as referring to unlawful marriages, i.e. those marriages which were seen, by the rabbis, as invalidly contracted.

Paul's Teaching on Christian Marriage

In his first letter to the Corinthians, St. Paul gives extensive teaching on Christian marriage.

1. The married should stay together: "A wife must not separate from her husband." (7:10)
2. If separated, the spouse cannot remarry: "If she does separate she must either remain single or become reconciled to him again. Similarly, a husband must not divorce his wife". (7:11)
3. Marriage creates a life-long bond: "A wife is bound to her husband as long as he lives." (7:39)
4. The married couple should not withhold sexual activity from the other: "the husband should fulfill his conjugal obligations toward his wife, the wife towards her husband." (7:3)
5. Marriage is a legitimate choice for a believer: "To avoid immorality, every man should have his own wife and every woman her own husband." (7:2)
6. Marriage is an honorable vocation: "The man who marries his virgin acts fittingly." (7:38)
7. Death of one's spouse frees the other to marry again: "If her husband dies, she is free to marry again, but on one condition, that it be in the Lord." (7:39)

Church Annulments

1. For many centuries, the Catholic Church, in its pastoral concern, has taught that some marriage vows were not validly contracted due to some error or lack of intention in one or both of the parties.
2. This long tradition is part of modern Church law (promulgated in 1917 and again in 1983).
3. Every divorced Catholic, or a divorced non-Catholic who wishes to marry a Catholic, has a right to approach a Catholic Tribunal asking for an investigation into their marriage.
4. Because the Catholic Church has a much higher ideal of marriage than the state (for example, the parties must be open to children, etc.) the Church sees more marriages as invalid than the State.

SPECIAL ISSUES

Pre-Marital Sex

1. Today, birth control devices are freely distributed in public schools which give the wrong message - "Have sex but make it safe sex."
2. Modern television and movies presuppose that young people have sexual intercourse very early on, even in the most casual of relationships.
3. This cultural brainwashing fosters superficial relationships. The partners, although having sexual relations, have never sorted out their emotions and are blinded to the real issues they should be honestly facing.
4. Jesus demanded a higher ideal, asking a man not even to look with lust upon a woman. (Mt 5:28)
5. Pre-marital abstinence is no foolproof means of choosing the right marriage partner, but it certainly helps to avoid choosing the wrong partner (and saves a lot of devastating emotions).

Artificial Insemination

1. The Church wants couples to have children.
2. However, the Church does not accept every means of conception as morally acceptable.
3. "Techniques that entail the dissociation of husband and wife, by the intrusion of a person other than the couple (donation of sperm or ovum, surrogate uterus) are gravely immoral." (Cat. 2376)
4. These means "betray the spouse's right to become a father and a mother only through each other." (2376)
5. Other techniques "involving only the married couple . . . are perhaps less reprehensible yet remain morally unacceptable." (2377)
6. These techniques are called "homologous artificial insemination and fertilization". (2377).
7. They dissociate the "sexual act from the procreative act" and "establish the domination of technology over the origin and destiny of the human person." (2377)

Denial of Sexual Relations

1. One of the greatest sins is the breakdown of marital relations between husband and wife.
2. A loving relationship in marriage is impossible to sustain without sexual relations.
3. When a spouse quietly withdraws from having sexual relations, a cycle is established which gradually destroys the interpersonal relationship.
4. The first step to restoration is to communicate about the issues that caused the breakdown in the first place.
5. Sharing in religious worship should be a help to better communication and to a healthier sexual life.
6. Even if there is infidelity the Church recommends that the partner, in Christian charity and for the family good, pardon their guilty spouse and continue having sexual relations. (C.1152 #1)
7. However, the Church law states clearly that the spouse can refuse marital relations if the adultery has not been consented to, condoned or caused by the spouse and the spouse has been faithful to the marriage vows. (C.1152 #1)

Artificial Birth Control

1. No teaching of the Catholic Church is so controversial, so contradicted by other Christian denominations or so unaccepted by its own members as the Church's teaching against the use of artificial contraceptives in marriage.
2. This teaching is controversial because other Christian Churches changed their moral teaching. Before 1930, every Christian Church condemned contraception.

Effects of Birth Control

1. Rejecting the union of sexual pleasure with the duty of procreation leads logically to many other selfish sexual decisions.
2. A society imbued with a contraceptive-mentality inevitably becomes a sexually permissive society and a "culture of death" society.

3. Because of the contraceptive mentality, society now faces other serious moral questions: abortion, premarital and extra-marital sexuality and homosexuality and even euthanasia.

Natural Family Planning
1. The Church teaches that God has built into the woman's body a cycle of fertility and infertility. This cycle is God's plan for couples to choose to conceive or not to conceive.
2. Unfortunately, this Natural Family Planning approach is set aside because it requires sexual discipline and communication.
3. Many, however, are beginning to see the devastating effects of artificial means and the positive results of Natural Family Planning (NFP).
4. The most startling statistic is the extremely low divorce rate among couples using NFP.
5. Artificial contraception breeds divorce because couples have little need to communicate or to abstain out of concern for the other party or for the good of the family. Selfishness grows and a huge divorce rate ensues.

Other Evils from Contraception
1. The contraceptive mentality also leads to abortion, which is seen as a legitimate means of birth control if contraceptive pills or devices fail.
2. Contraception encourages pre-marital sexual activity, since the normal deterrent of a possible pregnancy is removed.
3. Contraception totally changes lifestyles. Armed with contraceptives, unmarried couples feel quite free to live together, to vacation together (like a honeymoon couple) and to assume all the privileges of marriage, while refusing to accept the duties of married life. They have artificially removed the procreative aspect of their sexual relations.

Masturbation
1. A serious problem, especially for young unmarried men, is the temptation to seek sexual gratification alone.

2. Masturbation often results in a deep-seated feeling of guilt and emptiness. The person senses that they should be having some control.
3. The first step to purity is to avoid all erotic sources of stimulation. (This topic is treated under the Ninth Commandment.)
4. The second step is a regular use of the sacraments, especially Reconciliation.
5. The regular guidance of a priest-confessor, together with sincere efforts to remove external occasions, is the best, long-term approach.
6. The person should never see their sexuality as evil.
7. By the virtue of chastity the person realizes that sexual desires should not go uncontrolled and takes the needed steps to live as purely as possible.

Homosexuality – Scriptural Teaching

1. Although the word "homosexual" or "homosexuality" is not used in the scriptures, many texts do speak about this sin. (The 1986 NAB translation does use the words "practicing homosexuals" instead of "sexual perverts" 1TM 1:10)
2. Homosexual activity is associated in the Bible with the city of Sodom. Lot is saved by two angel visitors whom the citizens of Sodom wanted for homosexual activity. (Gen. C19)
3. Paul writes, "Do not deceive yourselves: no sodomites ... will inherit God's Kingdom." (1Cor 6:9-10 cf also 1Tim 1:10)
4. Paul's condemnation of homosexual activity is even more explicit in Romans: "Their women exchanged natural intercourse for unnatural, and the men gave up natural intercourse with women and burned with lust for one another." (1:26-27)

Church's Teaching

1. The Church's Catechism (2357-59) states the following:
   a) All unjust discrimination against homosexuals should be avoided.
   b) Like every Catholic, homosexuals are called to chastity.

c) They must use prayer and the sacraments to gain the needed inner freedom.
d) Under no circumstances can homosexual acts be approved.

Sources of Homosexual Attraction

1. Every person, beginning at birth, passes through stages of sexuality.
2. In some of these early stages, the attraction is toward members of the same sex.
3. Most pass through these stages and grow to a heterosexual orientation.
4. For many reasons yet unknown, the homosexual person finds himself/herself drawn to members of the same sex.
5. This process of sexual identification goes on quite unconsciously.
6. The Church states clearly, "They do not choose their homosexual condition."

What Can Be Done?

1. The power of homosexuality varies greatly from person to person.
2. Some say that, through therapy and Christian prayer, they have come out of a homosexual orientation.
3. Every believer must trust that God will provide, as only He can, all that is needed to live chastely.
4. God provides much help, but the person will only discover these if they are committed to a chaste lifestyle.
5. The homosexual person is asked to live the same as a heterosexual person who never marries.

The Church's Approach

1. A homosexual orientation does not preclude a deep Catholic life, and has often been used by God as an occasion for His greatest graces.
2. The Church invites homosexuals to remain close to the sacraments, the source of chastity for all Catholics.
3. Homosexuals should find a confessor to whom they go regularly for the Sacrament of Reconciliation.

4. In this sacrament, they can experience Christ's forgiveness and the Church's encouragement to holiness.

CONCLUSION

1. Training for chastity must begin early, with parents communicating ideals, and safeguarding their children from harmful sexual stimuli.
2. As young people enter puberty, they must begin their own struggle. This struggle is extremely difficult and prolonged, but very important.
3. This struggle focuses on controlling inner thoughts and desires, avoiding external sources of sexual enticement, as well as avoiding impure acts.
4. A sincere seeking of personal chastity will help the person to avoid promiscuity (having sexual activity with many partners).
5. This searching should also lead the person to avoid pre-marital sex, having sexual acts with one person with whom there is some relationship.
6. Avoiding pre-marital sex is important, because selecting the right person to marry is a difficult task which becomes complicated by sexual acts.
7. Sexual activity doesn't prepare the person to be a good spouse, whereas, purity is excellent training for a good sexual relationship in marriage.
8. These issues concerning sexuality are extensive and much more can be written. (My previous booklet entitled "The Seven Sacraments", commented on many issues relating to Matrimony.)

SEVENTH COMMANDMENT

"You shall not steal."

The Basic Command
1. The commandment, "You shall not steal." is given in three texts of the Old Testament. (Ex. 20:15; Lv.19:1 and Dt. 5:19)
2. Jesus, when asked what commandments should be kept to enter eternal life, said, " You shall not steal." (Mt.19:18, also Mk. 10:19 and Lk. 18:20)
3. Paul asks his Jewish readers, "You who preach against stealing, do you steal?" (Rom. 2:21) and he lists among the commandments, "You shall not steal." (Rom. 13:9)
4. Paul writes clearly, "The man who has been stealing, must steal no longer." (Eph. 4:28)

Definition
1. Stealing is taking what someone else owns against their reasonable will.
2. Every person has a right to own, which must be respected by everyone else.
3. If theft is the only means available to provide for immediate, essential needs (food, shelter, clothing), then the will of the owner to retain goods for himself is unreasonable.
4. This commandment requires restitution, a restoring of what has been stolen.

Avarice (The Deep Problem)
Stealing is rooted in avarice, a love for riches. The following texts confront the problem of avarice.

Old Testament
1. "He who trusts in his riches will fall." (Pr.11:28)
2. "This is a grievous evil, which I have seen under the sun: riches kept by their owner to his heart." (Eccl.5:12)
3. "Keeping watch over riches wastes the flesh." (Sir.1:1)
4. "Your heart has grown haughty from your riches." (Ez. 28:5)

Jesus' Teaching

1. Jesus is very clear that riches block the entrance to the Kingdom:

    a) "I assure you, only with difficulty will a rich man enter the Kingdom of God." (Mt.19:23)

    b) "Woe to you rich, for your consolation is now." (Lk.6:24)

2. Jesus condemns avarice in:

    a) the rich man with the gigantic harvest who "grows rich for himself instead of growing rich in the sight of God" (Lk.12:21)

    b) the rich man refusing to feed the beggar Lazarus who sat at his gate (Lk.16: 19-31)

3. Jesus taught that riches ruined the power of God's word:

    a) "Their progress is stifled by the cares and the riches and pleasures of life and they do not mature." (Lk.8:14)

Paul's Teaching

Paul has the same warning:

1. "Those who want to be rich are falling into temptation and a trap." (1Tim.6:9)

2. "Tell those who are rich in this world's goods not to be proud and not to rely on so uncertain a thing as wealth." (1Tim.6:17)

Full Extent of Avarice

Direct stealing, taking what belongs to another, is clearly seen as wrong. However, there are many other, more serious methods of stealing which are truly destructive of individuals and society.

Softening the Burden

1. The Old Testament commanded many initiatives to soften the burden of the poor:

    a) jubilee year (Lev. C25)

    b) prohibition of usury (Neh.5:10)

    "I myself, my kinsmen, and my attendants have lent the people money and grain without charge. Let us put an end to this usury."

    c) rules about the gleaning of fields (Lv.19:9)

2. Concerning this gleaning, Boaz "instructed his servants to let Ruth glean among the sheaves themselves without scolding her, and even to let drop some handfuls and leave them for her to glean." (Ruth2:16)

New Testament Examples of Changed Attitudes
1. The New Testament has examples of changed attitudes toward acquired wealth.
2. Zaccheus, when Jesus said He would come to his house, suddenly sees all his wealth in a different light. "I give half my belongings, Lord, to the poor. If I have defrauded anyone in the least, I pay him back fourfold." (Lk.19:8)
3. The Jerusalem believers, touched by the Pentecostal Spirit, made serious changes in their economic system. "Those who believed shared all things in common; they would sell their property and goods, dividing everything on the basis of each one's need." (Acts 2:44-45)

Immediate Action
1. Without waiting for needed worldwide economic changes, every believer who is truly touched by the Spirit of Jesus, needs to make a radical shift in their use of money.
2. Every believer must realize that, although they earned their riches, and rightly consider these goods private property, these goods belong basically to the whole human race. Giving away surplus money is not charity, but justice.

Business Practices
1. Scripture condemns unjust practices: "You shall not keep two differing weights in your bag, one large and the other small, nor shall you keep two different measures in your house, one large and the other small. But use a true and just weight and a true and just measure." (Dt.25, 13-15)
2. Showing that this is an important issue, Deuteronomy concludes "Everyone who is dishonest in any of these matters is an abomination to the Lord, your God." (V 16)

Fair Wages

1. Access to employment must be open to all without unjust discrimination. (Cat. 2433)
2. An employer cannot take advantage of the economy. Even if the laborer agrees to his salary, it might still be an unjust wage. (Cat. 2434)

Fair Wages in Scripture

1. Both Old and New Testaments condemn taking advantage of workers.
2. "You shall not defraud a poor and needy hired servant." (Dt.24:14)
3. "You shall not withhold overnight the wages of your day laborer." (Lv.19:13)
4. "Here, crying aloud, are the wages you withheld from the farm hands who harvested your fields. The cries of the harvesters have reached the ears of the Lord of hosts." (James 5:4)

Unbridled Capitalism

1. The greatest task of mankind is a total and complete remaking of the present world economic system.
2. God intended that the goods of this world be owned by the whole human race.
3. Everything really belongs to everyone.
4. An economic system which accepts the right of persons to own is morally acceptable.
5. However, all goods retain their primary goal of aiding all peoples.
6. Unfortunately, "private ownership thinking" so dominates the world markets that no one accepts in practice this primary truth of all mankind really owning everything.
7. The greatest stealing in today's world is due to unbridled Capitalism based upon a false idea of private ownership.

Almsgiving

To counteract the inner tendency to avarice, and to correct social inequities, the Old Testament urges almsgiving.
1. "Give alms from your possessions." (Tb. 4:7)

2. "Alms atone for sins." (Sir. 3:29)
3. In the midst of his scathing condemnation of the Pharisees, Jesus suddenly interjects this thought: "If you give what you have as alms, all will be wiped clean for you." (Lk.11:41)
4. To His "little flock", Jesus gave this advice: "Sell what you have and give alms." (Lk.12:33)
5. Paul writes, "He who gives alms, should do so generously." (Rom.12:8)

OTHER PERSONAL SINS

Gambling
1. Gambling Casinos and state governments sinfully raise billions of dollars from those addicted and from those who need the money.
2. "The passion for gambling risks become an enslavement". (Cat. 2413)
3. What used to be marginal (illicit gambling, numbers, etc.) has now become part of mainstream America.
4. Christian justice and charity require excess money be given to the poor, and not be wasted in casinos.
5. Together with pornography, gambling is now accessible to all in mainstream contexts.
6. Governments have totally failed their people, embracing what used to be relegated to the criminal element, and using this addiction, to balance budgets.
7. Jesus' gospel teaching (and St. Paul's) asks that surplus income be given to the poor. Saying "I can afford to lose a certain amount of money at the casinos, or on the lottery," means the clear word of Jesus and the main point of many parables have had no effect.

Credit Card Debt
1. The Old and New Testament tell us not to steal, but with credit cards we can own what we cannot pay for.
2. Credit card companies love this "over buying" which allows them to steal by their exorbitant interest rates.

3. Credit card debt is the hole in the American wallet which leads to terrible decisions (like two or three jobs) which destroy homes and families.
4. Saddled with debts (college loans, purchases, mortgage) the young couple is not free to make decisions based on the family's good. Decisions are affected more by financial needs than objective truth.
5. The commandments call for greater simplicity of life. When children are not subjected to television advertising, parents are free from the "nag factor".

CATHOLIC TEACHING ON SOCIAL JUSTICE

The Church has an extensive Social Justice teaching. The following presents the official teaching of the Church from its own Catechism:

Basic Catholic Principles
1. The Church has always taught the right of private ownership.
2. The Church, however, also teaches that "the goods of creation are destined for the whole human race." (Cat. 2402)
3. The conclusion is, "the right to private property ... does not do away with the original gift of the earth to the whole of mankind." (Cat. 2403)
4. Therefore, private ownership is secondary to the primary ordering of the earth for all people's benefit. "The universal destination of goods remains primordial." (Cat. 2403)
5. "Political authority has the right to regulate the right of ownership for the sake of the common good." (Cat. 2406)
6. All of the above leads to important conclusions in the economic sector.

Role of the State
1. Because of human selfishness, economic activity cannot be left totally in the hands of the rich.
2. Profit cannot be the exclusive norm of a business activity. (Cat. 2424)

3. The marketplace cannot be the only determining factor. Reasonable regulation is always needed so the common good is safeguarded. (Cat. 2431.)

Communism and Capitalism
1. The Church has "rejected totalitarianism which is associated with Communism or socialism". (Cat. 2425)
2. The Church has "refused to accept, in the practice of capitalism, ... the absolute primacy of the law of the marketplace over human labor." (Cat. 2425)
3. A regulation of the marketplace is always needed for the common good. (Cat. 2425)

Duties of Rich Nations
1. Inequality of resources "creates a real gap between nations." (Cat.2437)
2. The following "perverse mechanism" needs to be dismantled:
   a) the usurious financial systems
   b) the commercial relations that do damage to nations that are left out
   c) the arms race, which diverts money from useful goals (Cat. 2438)
3. Rich nations have a duty in justice to help the poorer countries. (Cat. 2439)
4. This help should include "direct aid". (Cat. 2440)
5. Even more important, is reform of the financial institutions so that poor economies can grow. (Cat. 2440)
6. The task of social justice lies primarily with the lay faithful. (Cat.2442)

Conclusion
1. The world economy and economic structures are so complex that clear rules are seemingly impossible.
2. Every Catholic, who daily experiences and participates in this complex economic world, must seek to build economic policies and structures which benefit as many as possible.

3. The Church teaches clearly that lay Catholics should "act on their own initiative" so that just social action "can assume concrete forms". (Cat. 2442)
4. The Church wants to listen to lay Catholics so that patterns and concrete models of justice be provided to society.

EIGHTH COMMANDMENT

"Thou Shalt Not Bear False Witness Against Thy Neighbor"

Human Speech
1. The power to speak is uniquely human.
2. All human life depends upon this ability to communicate with one another.
3. Because this communication is so vital, each person must be honest in their speech.

Cause of Sin
1. The Bible traces all sin to a lie, spoken to Eve by the devil who wanted her to disobey God.

    "You certainly will not die! No, God knows well that the moment you eat of it you will be like gods who know what is good and what is bad." (Gen. 3:4-5)

OLD TESTAMENT

The Commandment
On three occasions, God clearly commands truth:
1. "You shall not bear false witness against your neighbor." (Ex.20:16)
2. "You shall not bear dishonest witness against your neighbor." (Dt. 5:20)
3. "You shall not lie or speak falsely to one another." (Lev. 19:11)

Truthfulness of God
The Bible constantly pictures God as true:
1. "You, our God, are good and true." (Wis. 15;1)
2. "You are God and your words are truth." (2Sam. 7:28)
3. "You have established the truth." (Ps. 119:90)
4. "The ordinances of the Lord are true." (Ps.19:10)
5. "David rejoiced in God's promise knowing that God's words are truth.'" (2Sam. 7:28)

The Truthful Person
The Psalms encourage us to seek the truth:
1. "Guide me in your truth." (Ps.25:5)
2. "Take not the word of truth from my mouth." (119:43)
3. "The way of truth, I have chosen." (119:30)

Wisdom Books
1. The Wisdom books provide guidance for our speech:
   a) "Another man's secrets do not disclose." (Prov. 25:9)
   b) "Rather be a poor man than a liar." (Prov. 19:22)
   c) "Better a thief than an inveterate liar." (Sir. 20:24)
2. These books provide motivation:
   a) "The false witness will not go unpunished and he who utters lies will perish." (Prov. 19:9)
   b) "The slanderer besmirches himself and is hated by his neighbors." (Sir. 21:28)
   c) "He who betrays a secret cannot be trusted." (Sir. 27:16)

Power of the Tongue
1. "Death and life are in the power of the tongue." (Prov. 18:25)
2. "A man's tongue can be his downfall." (Sir. 5:15)
3. "Happy is he who sins not with his tongue." (Sir. 25:8)

The Story of Daniel and Susanna
The story of Susanna (Dan. C13) highlights the sin of using words to escape punishment, while falsely accusing another. This simple story focuses on both purity and truth:
1. Two elders, appointed judges in Israel, lusted for Susanna but she refused their approaches.

2. They claim that they caught her in adultery.
3. Daniel, however, proves that the two men are lying.
4. Susanna lives and the two men are killed.

NEW TESTAMENT

Jesus' Teaching
1. Jesus accepts the Old Testament teaching:
   "You have heard the commandment imposed on your fore-fathers, 'Do not take a false oath, rather, make good to the Lord all your pledges.'" (Mt. 5:33)
2. Jesus goes beyond this basic teaching:
   "What I tell you is: do not swear at all. Say 'Yes' when you mean 'Yes' and 'No' when you mean 'No'. Anything beyond that is from the evil one." (Mt. 5:34 and 37)
3. By these words, Jesus requires our speech to be simple and true.

Jesus and Truth
John's gospel focuses on Jesus as the truth.

Jesus describes Himself:
"I am the way, the truth and the life." (14:6)
"I deal in the truth." (8:45)
"You will know the truth and the truth will set you free."(8:32)

Jesus describes the Holy Spirit:
"When he comes, however, being the Spirit of truth, he will guide you to all truth. (16:13)

Jesus describes His purpose:
The reason I was born, the reason why I came into the world, is to testify to the truth." (18:37)

Jesus wants truth in His disciples
"Consecrate them by means of truth. Your word is truth." (17:7)

Book of James
James highlights the importance of the tongue:
1. "If a person is without fault in speech, he is a man in the fullest of senses." (3:2)

2. "The tongue is a small member, yet it makes great pretensions." (3:5)
3. "The tongue, no man can tame." (3:8)

Satan and Lies

The Bible reveals a close connection between Satan and lying.
1. Satan deceives Eve. (Gen 3: 1-7)
2. Jesus calls Satan, "the father of lies". (Jn. 8:24)
3. Peter says that Ananias' lying is caused by Satan: "You let Satan fill your heart so as to make you lie to the Holy Spirit..." (Acts5:3)

When We Are Liars

John calls us "liars" on four occasions.
1. If we continue to walk in darkness (1:6)
2. If we say we have never sinned (1:10)
3. If we deny that Jesus is the Christ (2:22)
4. If we proclaim to love God but hate our brother or sister (4:20)

PRACTICAL APPLICATIONS

Lying

1. By lying, we misuse human speech which God gave us to communicate truth.
2. The reasons for lying are many:
   a) to gain some selfish advantage
   b) to harm another person
   c) to shift blame away from ourselves

Power of Lies

1. Lies subvert all human relationships – whether personal, corporate or political.
2. The most destructive human systems of the 20th century, Communism, Nazism, Fascism, were built upon lies.
3. As shown above, there is a direct connection in the Bible between Satan's power and lies.

Other Ways to Misuse Speech

We can misuse speech in the following ways:

1. Detraction – revealing another's faults (even though true)
2. Slander (calumny) – harming a person's reputation by telling faults that are not true.
3. Flattery or Adulation – using words to ingratiate ourselves
4. Boasting (bragging) – exalting ourselves
5. False praise – confirming someone in their evil ways
6. Keeping silent – when duty calls us to speak up
7. Perjury – lying under oath

Keeping Secrets

1. Some secrets must be kept, no matter what it costs the person. These would include:
   a) the secrets of the confessional
   b) professional secrets revealed to priests, counselors, authorities, etc.
   c) even private secrets – when revealing them would do harm

Mass Media

1. With its astounding power to influence, the mass media has a very serious responsibility to truthfulness.
2. The mass media does not have a total right to reveal all the information it receives.
3. The media has to weigh its responsibility for the common good and the individual's right to a good reputation.
4. The media must present a complete and truthful picture.
5. Bias in reporting, so common in the media, is totally wrong and destructive of our society.

Truth in Public Life

1. Unfortunately, our political and economic worlds seem rooted more in lies than in truth.
2. The American people realize that politicians and governments frequently lie.
3. Large corporations are forced by the courts to pay huge sums to customers who have been lied to.
4. Our society does not even believe that an objective truth exists.

5. Isaiah, in his famous text, pleaded with the Israelite leaders, "Come now, let us set things right, says the Lord." (1:18) However, there can be no "setting things right' without a cultural foundation of truth.

Personal Witness to the Truth
1. By this commandment, believers must share their faith in Jesus.
2. Jesus said that a Christian witness will face persecution.
3. The believer must not fear because, "The Spirit of the Father will be speaking within you." (Mt.10:20)

NINTH COMMANDMENT

"You shall not covet your neighbor's wife." *(Ex. 20:17)*

Sixth and Ninth Commandment
1. By controlling sexual thoughts and desires, the person acquires a power over external actions.
2. These commandments requiring purity, both within and outside of marriage, present tremendous challenges to a Christian life.

The Challenge of Puberty
1. Between ten and twelve years of age, the human person enters puberty.
2. Before this age, nature provides a certain freedom from sexual drives. In this way, the child can mature.
3. This sexual maturing at puberty presents many new problems which are heightened by our very sexually oriented culture.
4. The most important cultural factor is the home, where, hopefully, the pubescent can experience the mature love of parents and needed guidance.
5. Unfortunately, this important cultural help has, in many cases, been destroyed by a divorce or a breakdown of any true loving relationship.

6. Today, we realize that sexual adjustment and identity is a process which begins at birth and is deeply influenced by early childhood experiences.
7. Many children enter puberty poorly prepared by their early years.

Power of Original Sin
1. In every person, the power of original sin makes these natural desires a dominating power – "I see in my body's members another law at war with the law of my mind." (Rom.7:23) This is especially true of the sexual desires, which are so important for both the person and the human family.
2. Even though an inner war exists, the person by the grace of Jesus, can win the victory.

Integrating Sexuality into the Personality
1. An integrated sexual life means that sexual impulses are not falsely repressed nor are they inappropriately acted out.
2. With chastity, "knowing the rules" is not enough. The person needs God's help to be pure.
3. A Catholic receives tremendous helps from:
    a) the Holy Spirit received in Baptism
    b) the regular reception of Holy Communion
    c) the honesty and forgiveness in a confession of sins
    d) the inner touches of God called religious experiences
4. Chastity, in thought and desire, provides a true mental hygiene, a deep inner cleanness. Jesus spoke against both external acts and internal lust.

Catholic Teaching on Modesty
Although much Catholic teaching on modesty has been destroyed by our modern world, this Catholic wisdom should be clearly outlined.
1. With puberty begins the onset of sexual development. The young person experiences physical, emotional, and mental changes which are meant to lead to marriage.

2. These new sexual desires cannot be acted out, because they are meant for marriage. This sexual restraint requires an inner purity.
3. A Catholic should not foolishly enter into temptation or be a sexual temptation to others (in the way they speak, dress or act).
4. The sum total of these efforts is called modesty, a serious attempt to shut off sexual stimuli and to act purely towards others.

Effects
1. Practicing modesty is absolutely necessary in becoming a selfless adult.
2. If no effort is made to be modest, then the sexual cravings will take control, leading to sexual sins and sexual addictions.
3. Unbridled sexual cravings unleash selfishness, a focusing upon personal satisfaction and a destroying of true love for others.

The Struggle
1. Modesty is the safeguard of chastity. The struggle for both modesty and chastity is difficult and not always successful.
2. Being pure in the pre-marital years, is the best preparation for marriage.
3. Even the married person needs to practice modesty, especially regarding pornography.
4. This struggle, aided by God's Spirit and the Church's sacraments, is well worth the effort.
5. Young people might easily feel cheated when they see others indulging in sexual pleasures. However, sexual discipline in youth is tremendously repaid in adulthood.

Chastity – A Preparation for Marriage
1. Everyone experiences sexual thoughts and desires many years before they are culturally ready for marriage.
2. Therefore, keeping this commandment demands a personal resistance to inner sexual promptings for many years.
3. This struggle actually prepares the person to be a good sexual partner in marriage.

4. Pre-marital chastity prepares the person for <u>marital</u> <u>tenderness</u> which is so needed to make sexual relations a truly mutual enjoyment.

OLD TESTAMENT

The Old Testament speaks frequently of this inner struggle and the discipline that is so desperately needed.

Problem From the Beginning
1. The problem of inner sexual rebellion happened early.
2. Adam said to God,"I was naked so I hid myself." (Gen.3:10). God then realizes, "You have eaten, then, from the tree of which I had forbidden you to eat." (3:11)
3. Therefore, the first consequence of sin is sexual disorientation. Adam and Eve needed garments, which God made for them. (3:21).

Other Biblical Evils
1. The evils continue to multiply as the problem of lust reappears frequently in the Old Testament.
2. David lusts for Bahsheba, commits adultery, and then plans the death of her husband. (2Sam 11:2)
3. Solomon, by his lust for foreign wives, reintroduces pagan worship into Israel.

Wisdom Literature
Israel's wisdom literature gives a full picture of purity.
Sound Advice
1. "Avert your eyes from a comely woman; gaze not upon the beauty of another's wife." (Sir.9:8)
2. "Go not after your lusts." (Sir. 18:30)
3. "Lust not in your heart after her beauty." (Pr. 6:2)
Prayer for Purity
1. "Let not the lustful cravings of the flesh master me." (Sir.23:6)

A Pure Example
1. Tobit, because of his purity, is able to overcome the demon that killed the previous husbands of Sarah. "You know Lord, that I take this wife of mine not because of lust but for a noble purpose." (Tob.8:7)

NEW TESTAMENT

The New Testament is even clearer on the need for inner purity of thought and desire.

Jesus' Sayings
1. Jesus affirms the sixth commandment, "You shall not commit adultery". (Mt.5:27)
2. Then, Jesus goes further saying: "Anyone who looks lustfully at a woman has already committed adultery with her in his thoughts." (Mt.5:28)
3. Jesus asks His disciples to focus on the inner sources of impurity, "From the mind stems evil designs . . . " (Mt. 15:19)
4. Jesus condemns those who don't cleanse their thoughts. "You cleanse the outside of the cup and dish, and leave the inside filled . . . with lust." (Mt.23:45)

ST. PAUL'S TEACHINGS
Purity in Speech
1. "As for lewd conduct or promiscuousness or lust of any sort, let them not even be mentioned among you." (Eph.5:3)

Need for Discipline
1. "Turn from youthful passions and pursue integrity." (2Tim.4:8)
2. "My point is that you should live in accord with the Spirit and you will not yield to the cravings of the flesh." (Gal.5:16)
3. "It is obvious what proceeds from the flesh: impurity, licentious ... and the like." (Eph.5:19-21)

Need for the Holy Spirit
1. Paul sees inner purity as a gift from the Holy Spirit within the believer.
2. "The fruit of the Spirit is . . . chastity." (Gal.5:22)

3. "The demands of the law might be fulfilled in us who live ... according to the Spirit." (Rom.8:4)

THE PROBLEM OF PORNOGRAPHY

Sources of Pornography
1. In recent years, pornography has become a gigantic moral problem, even for Catholics with strong ideals.
2. Pornography is especially troublesome for two reasons:
    a) This addiction takes control very quickly.
    b) Everyone can become addicted.
3. Pornographic addiction is especially widespread among men because of the nature of the male sexual drive.
4. Pornography is now available in socially acceptable ways through videocassettes, and pay-per-view channels.
5. Almost every hotel in America, in the secrecy of the room, provides pornography.
6. The greatest source of pornography is the Internet, whose use will constantly increase.

Effect Upon Marriages
1. For a married person, pornography is also a sin against their spouse, who is supposed to be the only source of sexual pleasure.
2. This addiction will ruin many marriages because the spouse is no competition for porno stars. The addicted person experiences a lessening of sexual desires for the spouse.
3. Sexual relations deteriorate and the bonding of marriage suffers when pornography becomes the sexual stimulant of choice.

Effects Upon the Young
1. Pornographic addiction destroys the young person, making the fantasy world more real than social relationships and interfering with decisions about a marriage partner.

THE PROBLEM OF TELEVISION

Getting Rid of the Problem

1. Two thousand years ago, Jesus spoke clearly to this point. After condemning lust, Jesus said, "If your right eye is your trouble, gouge it out and throw it away." (Mt.5:29) Because the eye that needs to be gouged out is the television, I propose the following guidelines:

2. If a home is to have a television, it should be in an out-of-the-way place.

3. Infants shouldn't be allowed near a television because their brain still needs to develop. American pediatricians ask for zero television watching before the second birthday.

4. The amount of television watching by all children of any age must be severely limited. (Scientists have been surprised to discover that the brain grows until age 15.)

5. In no circumstances, should any child under 18 be allowed to have a television in their room. (Consult new guidelines of American Pediatricians.) The same is true of the Internet.

The Need for a Radical Solution

1. Concerning the whole entertainment world, we must become radical. If the entertainment world is pulling for total freedom of expression, we have to pull just as hard in limiting our involvement.

2. This radical evil of the entertainment world requires a radical Catholic response of greater withdrawal from its use.

3. Catholics for whom cable television is the door to pornography have a moral duty to cancel their cable. Jesus would say the same. There is a very real question. "Should Catholics even allow cable television to enter the home."

4. Our moral teaching on this whole issue of television, videocassettes, cable stations, pay-per-view, "R" rated movies, has been wimpy.

5. Most Catholics won't want to hear those suggestions but they must be written.

Moral Blindness

1. I weep over the blindness of American Catholics, even good ones, who allow into their homes, every single day, very strong, very fascinating programs which give their children ideas, images and values which are totally contradictory to what the parents are trying to teach.

2. My only advice is to pull the plug and have a much happier home (at least after you have weathered the initial protest of your children).

Conclusion

Sincere attempts to be pure in thought and word, and to refuse to allow the mass media's sexual bombardment to control the thoughts and feelings are the best safeguards for personal chastity.

TENTH COMMANDMENT

"You shall not covet your neighbor's goods."

Seventh and Tenth Commandment

The Catholic Church links these two Commandments, teaching clearly that the inner coveting and craving for what is not ours (Tenth Commandment) leads to stealing and dishonest practices (Seventh Commandment). The focus, here, is on the inner sins of greed, envy, avarice, and the sadness that overpowers those who seek what is not theirs.

TWO MURDERS

The Old Testament records two specific murders which flowed from envy and greed.

Cain and Abel (Gen.4: 1-16)

The Bible explains in detail the struggle within Cain:

1. "Cain greatly resented this (God's blessing of Abel) and was crestfallen." (V5)

2. God tries to get Cain to face the cause, "Why are you so resentful and crestfallen?" (V6)
3. God gives Cain another chance, "If you do well, you can hold up your head." (V7)
4. God even warns Cain, "but if not, sin is a demon lurking at the door". (V7)
5. God tells Cain that he can overcome the temptation, "his urge is toward you, yet you can be his master." (V7)
6. Unfortunately, this envy is not set aside. Cain kills his brother. (V8)

Ahab and Naboth (IKings, C21)
1. Although Ahab, King of Samaria, seemingly has everything, he envies the vineyard of Naboth. He offers to buy it but Naboth refuses. He will not sell "an ancestral heritage".
2. Ahab's wife, Queen Jezebel, detects her husband's sadness. She asks the cause and decides to kill Naboth.
3. Ahab goes along with the murder, which leads to great evil upon his household.

Conclusion
1. The biblical teaching is clear. Coveting a neighbor's goods leads to dark inner feelings, which cause major problems.
2. God warned the Israelites, after their victory, "Do not covet the silver or gold on them, nor take it for yourselves, lest you be ensnared by it." (Lev.7:25)

Envy, Avarice and Greed
The prophets denounce these inner feelings.
1. "They covet fields and seize them, houses and they take them." (Mic. 2:2)
2. Ezekiel prophesies against Edom: "I will deal with you according to your anger and envy." (Ez. 35:11)
3. Isaiah explains why God allowed the Babylonian Captivity: "Because of their wicked avarice, I was angry." (Is.57:17)

Wisdom Texts

1. Joshua's command to the Israelites before conquering Jericho was: "Be careful not to take, in your greed, anything that is under the ban". (Jos.6:18)
2. A very special text explains God's blessings upon the Maccabees because "there was no envy or jealousy among them." (1Mac.8:16)
3. "Envy and anger shorten one's life." (Sir:30:24)
4. "From those who envy you, keep your intentions hidden."(Sir.37:10)

Jesus' Teachings

Jesus spoke against greed and envy:

1. Jesus listed greed and envy as "wicked designs" which "come from the deep recesses of the heart." (Mk.7:22)
2. Jesus said, "Avoid greed in all its forms" because "possessions don't guarantee eternal life." (Lk.12:15)

Jesus praised poverty of spirit:

1. "How blest are the poor in spirit, the reign of God is theirs." (Mt.5:3 and Lk.6:70))
2. "I assure you this poor widow has put in more than all the rest." (Lk.21:34)
3. Jesus invited the young rich man to sell all and become his follower. (Lk.18)

Jesus condemned the rich:

1. "How hard it will be for the rich to go into the Kingdom of God," (Lk.18:24)
2. "Woe to you rich, for your consolation is now." (Lk.6:24)
3. Jesus told the parable of the rich man who refused to feed the beggar Lazarus. (Lk.16:19-30)

Jesus is very explicit:

1. "In the same way, none of you can be my disciples if he does not renounce all his possessions." (Lk.14:33)

Jesus' Magna Charta

In Mt.6: 24-34, Jesus teaches poverty of spirit:

1. Jesus begins by alerting us: "Where your treasure is, there your heart will be also." (V21)
2. He says a decision must be made, "No one can serve God and money." (V.24)
3. Choosing money as a master leads to anxieties and the person loses sight of what life is all about. (V.15)
4. Life must be based upon a trust in the heavenly Father (V.26-29)
5. Our heavenly Father cares for every human being in a special way. (V.30)
6. No one should worry about tomorrow. Take one day at a time. (V.34)

Paul and Peter

1. Paul denounces those who, refusing to acknowledge God, are filled with . . . "greed and envy." (Rom.1:29) He lists envy among the sins which precede "from the flesh" (Gal.5:21) and as coming from false teaching . (1Tim.6:4)
2. Peter denounces those whose "hands are trained in greed." (2Pt.2:14)

Amassing Wealth

1. Natural inclinations, such as the desire for food, drink and even sexual pleasure, can be satisfied.
2. Amassing wealth, however, has no natural limitations. It is the great sin of the human spirit.

TITHING

Antidote to Greed and Avarice

1. In His teachings, Jesus goes against this "urge to possess" asking us to give our goods away.
2. Every believer should give at least ten percent (tithe) to God's works and God's poor.
3. Others, who already have a true surplus, should give more. Ten percent is the biblical minimum.

4. This decision to "bless others with our wealth", is a Christian weapon against the tyranny of greed and envy.

God's Clear Command
1. "Each year you shall tithe all the produce." (Dt.14:21)
2. "If the place is too far (to bring produce), you may exchange the tithe for money." (Dt.14:24)

Examples of Greater Generosity
1. In the reform of King Hezekiah, the Israelites gave "a generous tithe of everything." (2Chr.31:5)
2. Tobit says explicitly, that besides his tithe of produce, he always gave "a second tithe in money." (1:7)

TITHING – (Giving 10% to God)

Promise of Blessing
1. Tithing leads to God's blessings:
   "Shall I not . . . pour down blessing upon you without measure." (Mal.3:10)

Radical Poverty of Jesus
1. Jesus' teaching is even more radical. At times He invited people to "go sell what you have and give to the poor." (Mk.10:21; Mt.19:21 and Lk.18:22)
2. The Acts of the Apostles shows that the Early Church in Jerusalem went beyond merely tithing:
   a) "Those who believed shared all things in common." (2:44)
   b) "nor was there anyone needy among them, for all who owned property or houses, sold them and donated the proceeds." (4:34)
3. Even those not called to the total poverty, will be judged by their giving. Jesus will say to us, "I was hungry and you gave me food". (Mt.25:35) or He will say, "I was hungry and you gave me no food." (Mt.25:42)

70

Antidote to Greed

1. The Bible explains and commands tithing. It is the main antidote to avarice.
2. People who tithe make a definite decision that God will control their money.
3. This brings an inner freedom within the home, where finances can become a source of anger.

What is Happening?

1. Americans are the richest Catholics in the world.
2. In our own hemisphere, millions of Catholic brothers and sisters in Mexico, the Caribbean and Latin America starve.
3. Our own American Church does not have enough resources, both in missionary areas and in established dioceses.
4. The picture is serious and grave. American Catholics must quickly learn to tithe.

Catholic Parishes – "Tithe of the Tithe"

1. Catholic parishes and dioceses should follow the Old Testament norm and give at least 10% of what they receive to poorer parishes and dioceses.
2. The Old Testament calls this the "tithe of the tithes".
3. Two biblical texts speak clearly of this obligation:
   "You are to make a contribution from them (the tithes of the people) to the Lord, a tithe of the tithes. (Nm.18:26)
   "The Levites shall bring the tithe of the tithes to the house of our God." (Neh.10:38)
4. Obedience to this clear command will release the divine blessings promised by Malachi. (3:10)

Being Generous

1. We cannot take any money with us at death but we certainly can send it on ahead of time: "I was hungry and you gave me food." (Mt.25:35)
2. Not to help others is spiritual foolishness.
3. Some people imagine that all they need to do is leave a generous will. The Bible never mentions a will but speaks of actions during our lifetime.

Urgent Situations
1. The poor of the world are dying while American Catholic believers have enormous surpluses.
2. Many Catholics received a free education, or one subsidized by the parish. Because of this education, they are financially successful. Those Catholic schools, or others, need help.
3. Making a financial contribution every night of your life will get you a good night's sleep and a heavenly reward.

————

CHAPTER 11

COMMANDMENTS & CONFESSION

Law and Sin
1. Although knowing the commandments is important, this knowledge must lead to a good life.
2. Even Jesus coming into the world was "for the rise and fall of many in Israel." (Lk.2:34)
3. Jesus himself states "If I had not come to them and spoken to them, they would not be guilty of sin. Now, however, their sin cannot be excused." (Jn.15:27)
4. Paul wrote clearly about the Ten Commandments, "Yet it was only through the law that I came to know sin." (Rom. 7:7)

Sin and Guilt
1. American culture hates guilt, doing its best to make morality very ambiguous and fuzzy.
2. However, guilt can be a healthy emotion. If a person does something wrong, they should feel guilty.
3. The purpose of guilt is to force a person to face what they have done, to stop doing it, and, if needed, to make some reparation (even as small as saying, "I'm sorry").
4. Scripture focuses on a removal of guilt by turning to God for forgiveness. "Though your sins be like scarlet, they may become white as snow." (Is.1:18)

5. Catholics have a special sacrament called Reconciliation, which facilitates this healthy process of receiving God's forgiveness. (The biblical basis for this sacrament is contained in my previous booklet, "The Seven Sacraments".)
6. Forgiving sin and removing guilt is Jesus' gift to everyone. Joseph was told to name the child Jesus because "he will save His people from their sins." (Mt.1:21)
7. Jesus told the disciples, "penance for the remission of sins is to be preached to all the nations, beginning in Jerusalem." (Lk. 24:27)

The Church
1. Jesus gave to His Church, His power to forgive sins.
2. On Easter Sunday evening, Jesus "Breathed on them and said, 'Receive the Holy Spirit. If you forgive men's sins, they are forgiven them; if you hold them bound, they are held bound.'" (Jn.20:23)
3. The same Catholic Church that teaches the Ten Commandments also provides a sacrament for the forgiveness of sins.
4. James declares, "If he (the sick Christian) has committed any sins, forgiveness will be his. Hence, declare your sins to one another and pray for one another, that you may find healing." (Jas. 5: 15-16)

The Sacrament of Reconciliation (Confession)
(A full teaching on Confession is in my booklet, "The Seven Sacraments".)
1. Whenever a believer turns to God in sincere repentance and faith, his/her sins are forgiven.
2. Jesus has given His Church a special sacrament to complete and to aid this inner sorrow.
3. St. James correctly says, "declare your sins" because the human power of speech is the usual way of seeking forgiveness.
4. Besides the therapeutic act of confessing sins, the Catholic hears from the Church, through her priest, the words, "I absolve you from all your sins, in the name of the Father and of the Son and of the Holy Spirit."

5. These words are very similar to the Baptismal formula, "I baptize you in the name, etc."
6. The Fathers of the Church call Confession "a second Baptism",

Priest as Confessor

1. For Catholics, the Ten Commandments and Confession (the Sacrament of Reconciliation) are deeply intertwined. They are the two helps which the Church gives Catholics in their daily struggle with sin.
2. The Ten Commandments give clear moral ideals which every person should follow.
3. The forgiveness of Sacramental Confession helps people when they fall short of these ideals.
4. Interestingly, the Catholic Church is faulted for even having sacramental confession:
    a) Some say there should be no need to seek forgiveness from a priest.
    b) Others claim that seeking forgiveness in confession is a license to keep sinning.
5. The Church sees sacramental confession as a help needed to forgive, to encourage Catholics and help them to continue the pursuit of holiness.

Priest as Father

1. Catholics call their priests "Father" because of their role as "father confessor".
2. Catholics have all the moral demands spelled out clearly for them and they also have access to a "father confessor" who can forgive, and encourage.
3. Telling sins to a priest releases the powerful hold of sin.
4. The secular world sees the wisdom of this approach. The world calls this "therapy", the speaking to a skilled person about the inner burdens.

Power of Sacramental Confession

1. Receiving absolution by the prayer of the Church reaches much deeper than a personal confession to God alone (although this also is certainly important).

2. The following are the good effects:
    a) Confession occasions those important moments when the person honestly examines his/her own sinfulness.
    b) The sacrament allows God's power to touch the inner psyche.
    c) The whole experience is like a second Baptism, with forgiveness being given in the name of the Trinity.
    d) After Confession, Catholics experience inner freedom because the sins are taken away.
3. Confession allows the priest to see the person's struggles and failures, and then, to offer encouragement.
4. Sometimes, people need to be confronted by the priest about the seriousness of their behavior.

Duties of the Penitent and the Priest
1. To receive this sacrament, the person (called the penitent) must examine their conscience in light of the Ten Commandments, to see what sins have been committed since their last good confession.
2. The penitent then tells the priest the length of time since their previous confession and the sins committed.
3. The priest responds, in light of what was said. He, then prescribes a penance and says the Church's prayer of absolution.
4. After receiving the sacrament, the penitent should close the door on the past and experience the inner joy of having sins and guilt removed.
5. The penitent also experiences a thankfulness to Jesus for forgiving the sins and a sincere desire to avoid sin in the future.

Monthly Confession
1. Pope John Paul II has asked Catholics to receive this sacrament at least once a month.
2. The effects of regular forgiveness of sins and the removal of associated guilt, have profound effects on the person.

Attitude of Priests

1. Priests are trained to forgive. Only on the rarest of occasions, does the priest withhold forgiveness.
2. Because the penitents have freely approached this sacrament, they are presumed to be coming in good faith.

Rome Document (February, 1997)

1. At the request of Pope John Paul II, Rome sent guidelines for hearing Confessions to all priests. This document gives a picture of how a priest confessor should approach his task. It states the following:
2. "The gift of reconciliation is the specific mission of the Church."
3. Confession is "a salvific event of the greatest importance."
4. "In this sacrament each person can experience mercy in a unique way."
5. The priest "should always keep in mind that the sacrament has been instituted for sinners."
6. Unless there is a contrary proof, the priest should take for granted "the penitent's good will to be reconciled with the merciful God."
7. Although there must be sufficient repentance, frequent relapse into sins does not in itself constitute a motive for denying absolution."
8. The confessor should not exact "humanly impossible absolute guarantees of an irreproachable future conduct."

Conclusion

1. The document, therefore, stresses the truth of moral criteria and sees a "progressive path" toward "union with God's will" through a regular use of confession.
2. In other words, God loves us right now just as we are but He loves us too much to allow us to remain just as we are.

CHAPTER 12

SINS OF AMERICA

Although much about our country is good, there is a dark side to America, which has increased in the final decades of the 20th century. As citizens, we should face these sins, doing all we can to bring repentance and change through our political leaders.

1. Weapon Sales

The United States is the world's leading supplier of weapons. In 1976, President Carter tried to address the problem, but four years later the sales were even greater. In the late 1990's, Latin America was quietly added to the nations that can now buy arms from us. We now sell to Latin America because our sales to Europe have decreased (cold war is over) and our sales to Asia have decreased (economic crises). Therefore, we needed a new arms market to help our trade deficit. Just who gets killed by all the arms we sell doesn't seem to be a moral question to our politicians and businessmen.

2. Population Policy

We have forced our views on contraceptives, sterilization and abortion (all under the phrases "women's rights" and "availability to health") through the United Nations. Constantly, Pope John Paul II has had to fight the United States' positions at U. N. sponsored conferences, saying that the focus should be on the development of economies, not on birth control and abortion.

3. Third World Debt

Much of this debt is tied to arm sales and loans made to corrupt governments. These governments acted against the will of the people and are now out of office. As a result, the people cannot possibly get out of debt. Also, the original loan has already been paid back many times over in interest.

4. Land Mines

The United States refuses to sign the treaty barring the use of land mines, even though, long after a war is over, civilians are killed and maimed by these mines.

5. Children Soldiers

As of this writing, the United States has refused to accept a global agreement that no one under 18 can be recruited as a soldier. As a result, many children in other nations are killing other children with semi-automatic guns.

6. Conduct of War

Since Vietnam, even though we have engaged in many regional wars, America has lost a miniscule number of servicemen. The reason is that we now conduct wars from the sky, not the ground. Although these air wars reduce our casualties (a blessing), the use of bombs on civilian targets violates the criteria for a just war (cf Catholic Just War Theory under the Fifth Commandment).

7. Economic Blockades

We use economic blockades to bring down regimes (like in Iraq and Yugoslavia). The blockade is often unsuccessful, and carried on for years. As a result, America commits genocide, where thousand of innocent people are killed because of lack of food, medicine and other items needed for survival. The goal does not justify this immoral means.. Economic blockades are so horrible (and so unsuccessful) that they seem inherently evil. The Pope has constantly spoken against this genocide which is an inevitable result when the blockade goes on for years.

8. Exportation of Pornography

The United States supplies two-thirds of the world's pornography. Our censorless society is now polluting millions of minds.

9. Tobacco Sales

American cigarette companies take advantage of trade laws meant to open foreign countries to American goods. These other countries are extremely vulnerable because they do not have in place

America's anti-smoking campaigns. Anyone visiting a foreign country, in Europe or Asia, is immediately struck by the number of people who smoke. The Marlboro Man rides high.

CHAPTER 13

DON'T MISS THE BIG ISSUES!

Jesus asked the possessed man his name, "Legion is my name", he answered. 'There are many of us.'" (Mk. 5:9) Unfortunately, "legion" correctly describes the number of important moral issues. Although mentioned before, they need to be highlighted with additional comments.

Abortion
1. We have gone from the very false claim in the late 1960's, that a million "back alley" abortions were being performed, to a fulfillment of that unfortunately "prophetic" claim. Each year, over one million children (one out of every four conceived) are aborted.
2. With the future coming of the "abortion pill" (which Pope John Paul has called "Cain, the killer of our brothers and sisters"), and the greater acceptance of this pill by doctors, the number of abortions will probably increase.
3. Two recent secular studies have shown that, with the right to abortion, women have sensed the need to support themselves. Men no longer feel responsible to support a pregnant woman.
4. The long lasting mental anguish within the woman and the man has been totally covered up by pro-abortion groups.

Artificial Contraception
1. The Church teaches that God has built into the woman's body a cycle of fertility and infertility. This cycle is God's plan for couples to choose to conceive or not to conceive. Unfortunately, this natural approach to implement a couple's decision is set aside, as of little value.

2. In its place, our culture supplies various artificial means with many side effects. Having set aside the possibility of procreation, the couple does not need to communicate or abstain from sexual relations.
3. Instead of helping marriages, artificial contraception has opened the door to mutual egoism which has destroyed sacrificial love, the only true foundation of a marriage.

Television and Internet
1. Thank God the Association of Pediatricians has advised:
    a) Absolutely no television watching for infants under two years.
    b) Older children should not have television in their rooms.
2. The great moral decline of the world is due to television, both its content and its pervasiveness.
3. Television no longer forms our culture but has become our culture.
4. A greater problem already exists with the Internet video games. Electronic experiences take the place of real-life interaction.
5. The constant external stimuli precludes the time a person needs each day to face inner feelings and make choices based on real life.

Credit Card Debt
1. The Old and New Testament tells us not to steal, but with credit cards we can own what we cannot pay for.
2. Please, get out of credit card debt as fast as possible. The banks are stealing your hard-earned wages.

Pornography
1. America is wired for pornography. The pornography business is booming and "porno stars" have become mainstream American heroes, now lecturing on college campuses.
2. Pornography is an addiction which anyone can fall into. The person is quickly caught up in unleashed emotions which they cannot control.
3. Pornography has already become a great destroyer of marriages.

Divorce
1. Over 50% of American marriages end in divorce, a result of many aspects of modern culture.
2. Modern culture no longer fosters life-long commitments. To survive in marriage, couples must choose a "counter-cultural" life style.
3. This approach requires that they worship together both in church and at home.
4. They must make a decision to tithe their income, and to follow all the Church's teaching on sexual morality.
5. They need support from other couples who share the same values.

Consumerism
1. Family life used to be defined by the number of children. (A 1964 Time Magazine defined Bobby Kennedy's large family as outdated and Lyndon Johnson's two-child family as modern.)
2. Now, American families have substituted things for children allowing the advertising world to redefine what constitutes "basic needs".
3. Rejecting this consumerist attitude with a deliberate decision to tithe provides a freedom from financial tyranny.

Pace of Life
1. Everything is too fast. Homes are invaded by outside demands. Parents are no longer in control. Society sets the tone. Family meals are a thing of the past. No true bonding, which requires time for others, takes place because this entails time together. Nobody is home alone.
2. Slowing down on Sunday is the best place to begin.

Lack of Family Prayer
1. Family life includes pain. Closeness often results in hurts and disappointments. Family prayer allows God to enter in.
2. Family prayer results in forgiveness, or at least a willingness to forgive, that regularly washes away the daily hurts. Otherwise, all the pain just builds up.

3. The American Catholic family was deeply influenced by Father Peyton and his family rosary, "The family that prays together, stays together".
4. Begin with the rosary, or any other form of prayer.

The Lord's Day
1. Nothing so characterized American life in the 1940's and 1950's as keeping the Lord's Day.
2. Sunday was totally different because the stores were closed, people were home, and life had a different pace.
3. Everyone got the message that the day belonged to God and our country belonged to God.
4. Now, we have "sold out". God is seen as unimportant, unable to get attention on His own day.
5. The first step to moral renewal (for the person, the family and society), is keeping the Lord's day holy.

The Occult
1. The occult has moved from the fringe to the mainstream.
2. Decades ago, most American weren't involved with psychics, fortunetellers, crystal balls, psychic healing, mind control and the hundreds of other varieties of the occult. Now, Satanism, satanic cults, satanic powers and teachings are everywhere.
3. Eastern religions with the pantheistic beliefs are pulling people away from the biblical God of Abraham, Isaac and Jacob. We are going backward, falling into religious confusion.
4. Now advertisers "market" religious and spiritual experiences. What they market is not biblical, and violates the first commandment against having strange gods.
5. All the sociological studies show that America is in the midst of a religious ferment. Unfortunately, this religious searching is opening many wrong doors.

KEY OF DAVID BOOKS AND TAPES

This booklet, "The Ten Commandments" is just the most recent of the books tapes and videos written and produced by Monsignor Walsh.

The following are some others which are available. The style is easy-to-read, the quality is excellent and the prices are always moderate.

SCRIPTURE

The Kingdom at Hand (292 pages)   *Price: $10.00*
A unique prayer book on St. Matthew's Gospel. The ideas are simple and clearly written. The reader experiences the power of the scriptural text itself.

RELIGIOUS EXPERIENCES

The Power of David's Key (195 pages)   *Price: $5.00*
Personal stories which teach and encourage prayer experiences.

CHARISMATIC RENEWAL

These books provide a strong foundation, both in Charismatic spirituality and Church teaching:

A Key to Charismatic Renewal in the Catholic Church (286 pages)
                                                    Price: $6.00
The book is known for its clear description of the Charismatic Movement and has become a worldwide classic (also in Spanish).

Lead My People   *Price: $4.00*
This is a manual for those who guide a prayer group, large or small. The manual is also helpful to everyone who participates in a weekly prayer meeting.

Prepare My People   *Price: $5.00*
This book contains eight chapters on the beginning Pentecostal experiences and chapters on spiritual growth after receiving these initial gifts.

Teach My People   Price: $4.00
This book is a companion volume to *Lead My People*. Its purpose
is to help leaders with the charism of teaching. It provides solid
material for Catholic teachings.

Keep the Flame Alive   Price: $5.00
The first eight chapters explain Catholic teaching so that Catholics
appreciate the traditions of their 2000-year historical Church. The
second section is a dictionary of Charismatic terminology. The
third part is a teaching on prayer tongues which shows how this gift
matures and leads into other charisms.

SUNDAY HOMILIES
Sunday Homilies   Price: $5.00
Since 1996, the Sunday homilies have been recorded and are
available (two per tape).

BOOKS OF STORIES
The following three books have forty chapters each and are filled
with stories:

Special Words Just For You   Price: $5.00
This book hopes to show everyone that God is active every day and
in every type of circumstance. Hopefully, the reader's eyes will be
opened to a fresh view of faith.

If God Wants a Steak, He Pays for a Steak   Price: $5.00
This book hopes to show everyone that the manifestations of the
Spirit are happening in the Catholic Church and are available to any
person who would seek and search for a full life in the Spirit.

To The Angel of the Church in Philadelphia   Price: $4.00
This book is a collection of thirty-two articles outlining the many
beginning stories of the Spirit's work in Philadelphia.

HISTORY OF EVANGELISM
What is Going On   Price: $8.00
Many Catholics are confused by the worldwide growth of Protestant
Pentecostalism. In just 189 pages, Monsignor Walsh provides a
clear view of the history and dynamism behind Protestant
Evangelism.